KU-024-272

RSPB

What's that
BIRD?

Rob Hume

DK

LONDON, NEW YORK, MUNICH, MELBOURNE, AND DELHI

DK LONDON
Senior Art Editor Jacqui Swan
Senior Editor Angeles Gavira
Editor Lizzie Munsey
Production Editor Tony Phipps
Production Controller Emma Sparks
Jacket Designer Laura Brim
Picture Researcher Evi Peroulaki
CTS Adam Brackenbury
Managing Art Editor Michelle Baxter
Managing Editor Camilla Hallinan
Publisher Sarah Larter
Art Director Philip Ormerod
Associate Publishing Director
Liz Wheeler
Publishing Director Jonathan Metcalf

DK DELHI
Deputy Managing Art Editor
Mitun Banerjee
Managing Editor Rohan Sinha
Deputy Managing Editor
Alka Thakur Hazarika
Senior Art Editor Ivy Roy
Designers Arijit Ganguly, Arup Giri,
Pooja Pawwar, Khundongbam Rakesh
Editors Megha Gupta, Priyanka Nath
DTP Designer Bimlesh Tiwary
DTP Manager/CTS Balwant Singh
Production Manager Pankaj Sharma

First published in 2012 by
Dorling Kindersley Limited
80 Strand, London WC2R 0RL

Penguin Group (UK)

8 10 9
023 – 178090 – Jan/2012

Copyright © 2012
Dorling Kindersley Limited

A CIP catalogue record for this book
is available from the British Library
ISBN 978-1-40539-350-8

Reproduced by Media Development
and Printing Ltd., UK
Printed and bound in China

Discover more at
www.dk.com

ABOUT THE AUTHOR

As a writer, editor, and identification expert, **Rob Hume** is much in demand for his expertise on birds. A lifelong birdwatcher, he worked for the Royal Society for the Protection of Birds (RSPB) for 35 years, and edited the RSPB's award-winning *Birds* magazine, which has a readership of 1.8 million, for 20 years. For several years he was on the editorial board of the influential *British Birds* magazine and chaired the British Birds Rarities Committee. Rob continues to be an active editor, for the RSPB and others.

Contents

Introduction

Birds are fantastic creatures. They are unique not because
they fly, or lay eggs, but because no other animal group has
feathers. This book will help you identify the birds you see
close to home and in easy-to-reach places. It provides simple
profiles for the most common birds, with straightforward
language and clear photos to highlight the key differences
between similar-looking species. Each species is marked by
distinctive shapes and colours, calls and songs. Some have
different colours according to age, sex, and season. This book
cannot cover all variations, but it gives you a good start. Living
life at a fast pace, birds enjoy relatively brief, energetic lives,
although some, such as Fulmars (40 years) and swans (25),
live longer. The world's greatest globetrotters, millions of birds
such as geese and terns migrate thousands of kilometres
twice every year. Easier to see and more abundant than
mammals, birds are the most accessible wild creatures. There
are no rules about watching birds; you just need enthusiasm,
an enquiring mind, a pair of binoculars, and a notebook. So
look around you and enjoy them!

Rob Hume

Identifying Birds

Learning to tell which bird is which needs time and practice, but that is all part of the fun. Identifying birds also requires discipline: don't leap to conclusions but look carefully for the features that prove your identification, such as colour, size, shape, specific patterns, or particular calls.

Size

This is hard to judge: two birds of the same length can appear to be different sizes if they are not the same shape. The size of very similar-looking birds may surprise you: a Great Black-backed Gull is not much longer than a Lesser Black-backed Gull, but side by side it seems "twice as big" – and it is twice the weight. For the waders shown here, size is the main distinguishing feature.

DUNLIN

BAR-TAILED GODWIT

REDSHANK

CURLEW

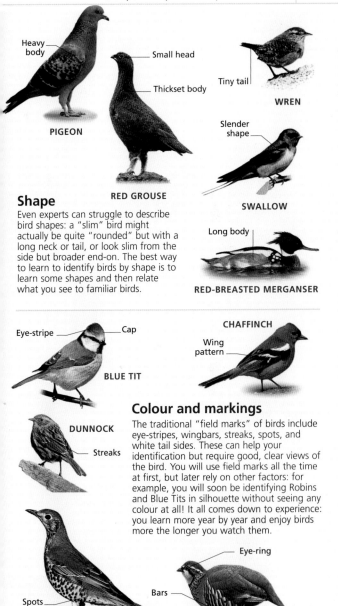

Heavy body

Small head

Thickset body

Tiny tail

WREN

PIGEON

Slender shape

RED GROUSE

Shape

Even experts can struggle to describe bird shapes: a "slim" bird might actually be quite "rounded" but with a long neck or tail, or look slim from the side but broader end-on. The best way to learn to identify birds by shape is to learn some shapes and then relate what you see to familiar birds.

SWALLOW

Long body

RED-BREASTED MERGANSER

Eye-stripe — Cap

CHAFFINCH

Wing pattern

BLUE TIT

DUNNOCK

Streaks

Colour and markings

The traditional "field marks" of birds include eye-stripes, wingbars, streaks, spots, and white tail sides. These can help your identification but require good, clear views of the bird. You will use field marks all the time at first, but later rely on other factors: for example, you will soon be identifying Robins and Blue Tits in silhouette without seeing any colour at all! It all comes down to experience: you learn more year by year and enjoy birds more the longer you watch them.

Eye-ring

Bars

Spots

MISTLE THRUSH

RED-LEGGED PARTRIDGE

Flight

Most small birds are difficult to identify in flight, as they dash past and dive into cover. Larger species provide more useful clues, and many big birds, such as birds of prey, spend long spells in the air. Some birds are quite easy to see in the air but are rarely (such as the Hobby) or never (Swift) seen on the ground.

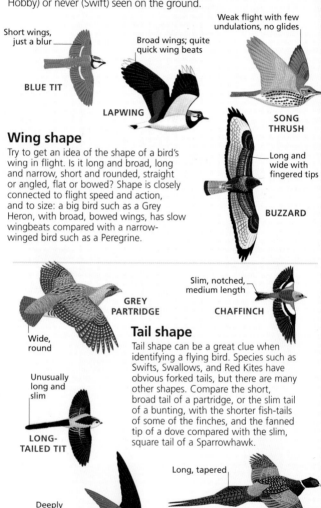

Short wings, just a blur

BLUE TIT

Broad wings; quite quick wing beats

LAPWING

Weak flight with few undulations, no glides

SONG THRUSH

Long and wide with fingered tips

BUZZARD

Wing shape

Try to get an idea of the shape of a bird's wing in flight. Is it long and broad, long and narrow, short and rounded, straight or angled, flat or bowed? Shape is closely connected to flight speed and action, and to size: a big bird such as a Grey Heron, with broad, bowed wings, has slow wingbeats compared with a narrow-winged bird such as a Peregrine.

GREY PARTRIDGE

Slim, notched, medium length

CHAFFINCH

Wide, round

Tail shape

Tail shape can be a great clue when identifying a flying bird. Species such as Swifts, Swallows, and Red Kites have obvious forked tails, but there are many other shapes. Compare the short, broad tail of a partridge, or the slim tail of a bunting, with the shorter fish-tails of some of the finches, and the fanned tip of a dove compared with the slim, square tail of a Sparrowhawk.

Unusually long and slim

LONG-TAILED TIT

Deeply forked

SWALLOW

Long, tapered

PHEASANT

Flight pattern

Size, shape, and flight action are closely linked, but some small, aerial birds (such as the Swift) glide and swoop like larger species, and some big, round-winged birds (like the Pheasant) have very fast beats. Try to describe what you see: fast, whirring flaps and undulations; slow flaps and floating glides; relaxed, "elastic" flaps compared with stiff, jerky beats, and so on. These diagrams show some of the different flight patterns you might come across.

wingbeats

Finch-like: sequence of short, fast bursts of beats between undulating glides

Woodpecker-like: bursts of beats between deep swoops with wings closed

Swallow-like: sideslips and swoops with fluid, relaxed wingbeats; bursts of wingbeats between glides

Duck-like: consistent, fast, deep wingbeats, without glides except when descending to land or water

Sound

Most birds are extremely vocal: they call to keep in touch. Some call loudly in flight, and many have loud, persistent songs with sounds and patterns characteristic of their species. You hear more birds than you see (and find most by hearing them first), so learning their sounds is invaluable as well as great fun. Many birds look so similar that listening to them is the best way to tell them apart.

GREENSHANK
Even, ringing *tew-tew-tew*

GOLDFINCH
Lisping, tinkling *skip-i-lip*

REDSHANK
"Bouncing", descending
tyew-yu-yu, teu, teu-hu

Season

Not all birds can be seen everywhere all year round. Some, such as Swallows and Cuckoos, are strictly "summer visitors" to the UK, arriving in spring and leaving in autumn. Others, such as Fieldfares and Bewick's Swans, arrive in autumn and spend the winter in the UK. Still others are seen only in passing on their migration in spring or autumn.

Wagtails

In winter, a wagtail with yellow under the tail will always be a Grey Wagtail, as the Yellow Wagtail is only present from April to October. No Yellow Wagtails spend the winter in northern Europe.

GREY WAGTAIL

YELLOW WAGTAIL

Pipits

The Meadow Pipit looks very similar to the Tree Pipit, but identification problems can be forgotten between October and March, when the Tree Pipit is in Africa.

TREE PIPIT

MEADOW PIPIT

Behaviour

It is easy to see differences in bird behaviour, even in the garden: look at the perky cockiness of a tail-flicking, head-bobbing, bold Robin compared with the quiet, shy shuffle of a Dunnock. Wherever you are, there will be birds with distinctive characteristics that are always worth learning. Use your own words to describe them: you will remember them more easily.

Dunnock

Sits upright to sing, but shuffles low and horizontally to feed, with little outward flicks of its tail feathers.

Great Tit

Quite "heavy" for a small bird; crashes about more than a Blue Tit and feeds on or near the ground more often.

Grey Heron

A waterside bird, but nests in treetops, and stands around in small groups for hours in dry fields.

House Sparrow

Sits on an obvious perch, flicking its tail, and cheeps. Also gathers in noisy, squabbling groups that bash about in hedges and thickets.

Treecreeper

Treecreepers are unable to stand or walk properly. They are strictly creepers on tree bark.

Parts of a Bird

Feathers are neatly arranged in particular groups, called tracts. In any species, the position, size, shape, and number of feathers in each tract are remarkably consistent.

Naming the parts

Using simple terms and names for the tracts, we can write a detailed description of any bird. Here, a Starling is shown perched and in flight, to show where the same feathers are in both positions. The labels on these Starlings show all you need to know to begin with. Some terms are further explained in the Glossary (p.125).

Cheek

Crown

Beak

Chin

Back

Chest

Wing coverts; pale tips may form bars on wing

Wingtips (fold over rump)

Tail (central and outer tail feathers)

Undertail coverts

Leg

Wingtips (primaries)

Eye-stripe

Underwing coverts

Hindwing (secondaries)

Tail

Undertail coverts

BIRD PROFILES

Starting close to home and then looking a little farther afield, these are the most common birds you can expect to see, grouped by habitat and then by appearance. Some birds can be seen in more than one habitat, but are dealt with here in the most likely one. Unless stated otherwise, where males and females look different, it is the adult male that is pictured.

Symbols
♀ Female
♂ Male
↔ Length

WREN
P.19

BLACKBIRD
Male, p.24

ROBIN
P.19

Garden

Flowers, shrubs, lawns, trees, and earth can make gardens a miniature mixture of other habitats. Some birds thrive in this patchwork, and more can be encouraged in by food, water, and the shelter provided by shrubs and trees.

1 CLOSE TO HOME

Habitats on your doorstep are often rich and varied: don't neglect the possibilities of gardens, town parks and ponds, and the nearest country park. You can often learn to identify common birds here before venturing further afield.

MALLARD
Male, p.62

MOORHEN
P.73

Pond or park lake

Wild ducks and waterbirds such as Mallards, Mute Swans, Moorhens, and several kinds of gulls easily take to suburban or even urban lakes – you never quite know what might turn up next.

House

If you are lucky, you may have birds on or around the house: House Sparrows, Starlings, and Swifts can be seen around homes, and House Martins even nest under the eaves of buildings.

HOUSE MARTIN
P.30

HOUSE SPARROW
P.18

Town centre

Even a city centre can offer a chance to see at least a few birds: Town Pigeons and maybe a Kestrel or a Peregrine overhead. There is also the chance of a Swift or two, and probably a Pied Wagtail.

TOWN PIGEON
P.28

KESTREL
P.54

Small Brown Birds

These small birds (all brown, except the Black Redstart) are seen around homes, offices, and gardens. You can tell them apart by looking at their shapes and movement.

DUNNOCK

Streaky brown and grey; darker than Robin, thinner beak than sparrow. Creeping, shuffly gait. Sits upright when singing its fast, warbling song.
↔ 14cm

Thin beak

Grey neck

Streaked back

Streaked sides

HOUSE SPARROW

Cheeky, chirruping, lively, and bold; a sociable bird of thickets, hedges, and buildings. Female is paler than male, with no black bib.
↔ 14cm

White bar on wing

Grey cap

Thick, triangular beak

Black bib

Plain underneath

TREE SPARROW

Similar to male House Sparrow but rare in gardens; found on farmland with old trees. Brown cap with no grey centre.
↔ 14cm

Black ear-spot

Brown cap

Black chin

Plain underside

What to look out for • Beak shape • Streaked or plain back • Face and cheek pattern • Hop, walk, or shuffle • Flicks of wings and tail

ROBIN

Small and cocky, with hop-hop-stop-and-look action. No red on young birds. Often sings loud, warbling song under lights at night.

↔ 14cm

Bold, dark eye

Pale, orange-red breast

Plain brown back

Flicks tail and wings

WREN

Tiny, feisty, barred brown bird of low, dense vegetation. Its short tail is often cocked up. Loud, trilling and warbling song.

Short, thin, stiff tail

↔ 9–10cm

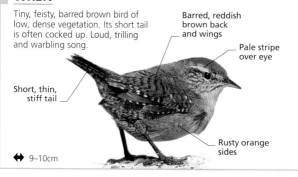

Barred, reddish brown back and wings

Pale stripe over eye

Rusty orange sides

BLACK REDSTART

Robin-like form, but much darker colour; females are grey. Often seen on rooftops in villages. Makes scratchy noise like grating stones.

↔ 14.5cm

Pale wing panel

Dark, rusty red tail

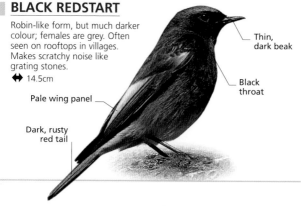

Thin, dark beak

Black throat

Finches

These sparrow-like finches have thick beaks and forked tails. Their beak shapes vary depending on what they eat. Some use feeders; others eat food spilled from them.

GOLDFINCH

Slender and sharp-beaked, with striking face pattern and yellow-banded wings. Found in small groups on thistles and other weeds.

↔ 12.5–13cm

White cheek and neck

Dark red face

Yellow across black wing

Forked tail, visible in flight

GREENFINCH

Stocky, unstreaked, and big-beaked, with yellow wing and tail flashes. Often found on feeders. Sings loud trills from treetops.

↔ 15cm

Thick, pale beak

Dark eye-patch

Yellow edge to wing

Unstreaked, dull green underside

SISKIN

Much smaller than Greenfinch, with black cap and bars on wings. Often found on birdfeeders or in tall trees with seeds and cones.

↔ 12cm

Black cap

Streaked green back

Yellow on neck and breast

Yellow flashes on tail and wing

What to look out for • Beak size and shape • Streaked or unstreaked above and below • Shape and colour of bars on wings • Rump and tail patches

CHAFFINCH

Sparrow-sized and unstreaked, with slim, notched tail and bold, white wing marks. Male pinkest in spring, dull-headed in winter. Female drab but same pattern. Bright, rattling song.

↔ 14.5cm

Blue cap

White shoulder patch

White bar on wing

Unmarked, pale pink underside

BULLFINCH

Stocky, upright, and colourful, with square white patch on rump; female is duller but same pattern as male. Secretive but makes loud, flat, simple whistle.

↔ 15cm

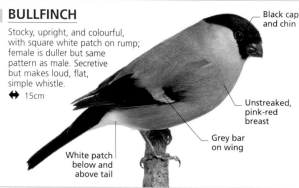

Black cap and chin

Unstreaked, pink-red breast

Grey bar on wing

White patch below and above tail

BRAMBLING

Shape like Chaffinch but has orange wing and breast patch with a white belly. Blacker head and beak in summer. Often found under beech trees.

↔ 14.5cm

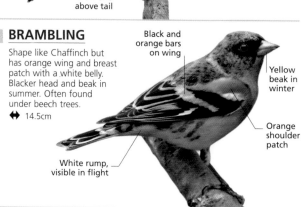

Black and orange bars on wing

Yellow beak in winter

Orange shoulder patch

White rump, visible in flight

Thrushes

These ground- or berry-feeding birds hop around on the grass, flying up to trees if disturbed. They may gather in groups outside the breeding season.

What to look out for • Streaks, stripes, or spots beneath • Head pattern • Plain or pale-streaked wings • Rump/tail contrast

SONG THRUSH

Small, speckled thrush of woods, lawns, and gardens. Plain back, wings, and tail. Song repeats each phrase several times.
↔ 23cm

Faint head pattern

Brown wing feathers

V-shaped spots on chest and sides

Plain brown tail

MISTLE THRUSH

Big, bold, upright thrush that makes long, leaping hops on ground. Loud, repetitive song and dry, chattering call.
↔ 27cm

Pale eye-ring

Pale edges to wing feathers

Bold spots on chest and sides

White edge to tail

REDWING

Small, dark, sociable thrush.
Often gathers in flocks in fields,
scarcer in gardens. Thin *seep* call.
↔ 21cm

Broad, pale
stripe over eye

Pale stripe
under cheek

Reddish patch
under wing

Streaked
underneath

FIELDFARE

A large, striking thrush with grey on its head
and rump. Often gathers in wandering
flocks. Chuckling *chak-chak* calls.
↔ 25cm

Yellow
beak

Grey patch
above
black tail

Black
around
eye

Black spots
on chest
and sides

BLACKBIRD ♀

Familiar garden and woodland thrush.
Female is brown with subtle, dark spots
beneath. Runs, hops, and feeds on
ground and in bushes.
↔ 24–25cm

Dark, smoky brown
back, rump, and tail

Yellow or
blackish
beak

Throat
spotted or
streaked

Underside
much darker
than Song
Thrush

♂ p.24

Medium-sized Garden Birds

These birds include a black thrush and a blackish starling, both likely to feed on lawns; a rare and exciting garden visitor; and a bold, opportunistic, piebald crow.

BLACKBIRD ♂

Familiar garden and woodland thrush. Often raises tail slowly after a short run. Pulls worms out of lawns. Loud, musical song; *pink pink!* alarm and *chook* calls.

↔ 24–25cm

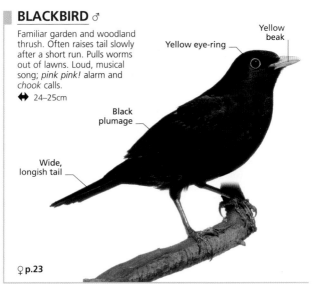

Yellow beak

Yellow eye-ring

Black plumage

Wide, longish tail

♀ **p.23**

STARLING

Spotted or mottled, short-tailed, busy bird. Walks on the ground and has fast, sharp-winged flight. Rattles and whistles in song. Huge flocks look like smoke clouds from a distance.

↔ 21cm

Sharp, yellow beak

Glossy black body with green and purple sheen

Long, strong, red-brown legs

Short, square tail, kept down

What to look out for • Tail length and shape • Spotted or unspotted plumage • Crest or no crest • Feeding actions

WAXWING

Starling-like shape but dumpier. Unique crest on head. Often very tame. Visits in winter, stripping trees of berries. Flocks rest in trees between bouts of feeding. Call a high trill.

⟷ 18cm

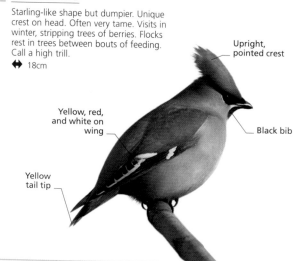

Upright, pointed crest

Yellow, red, and white on wing

Black bib

Yellow tail tip

MAGPIE

Big, black-and-white bird, with long tail. Often gathers in groups that make loud, clattering calls. Builds big, untidy nests that are obvious in winter when leaves fall.

⟷ 44–46cm

Black head and chest

Big, white shoulder patch

Long, glossy, green-purple tail

White underneath

Blue Tit & Relatives

These tiny, acrobatic, and boldly marked birds often
come to feeding stations and bird tables, but are
equally at home in woods and hedgerows.

What to look out for • Yellow, green, or blue colour on
body • Head pattern • Underside colour, especially on chin
or throat • Tail shape

GREAT TIT

A small, agile bird with striking head pattern.
Common in gardens and woodlands; often seen
on feeders. Strident, two-note *tee-cher* song.

↔ 14cm

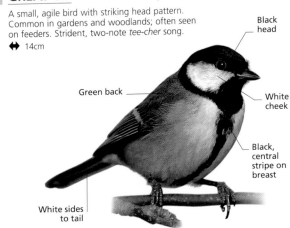

Black head

Green back

White cheek

Black, central stripe on breast

White sides to tail

BLUE TIT

Greenish or yellowish bird with
white face. Blue cap, wings, and tail
seen at closer range. Fairly tame and
noisy; often found on feeders.

↔ 11.5cm

Blue cap

Dark stripe on white face

Grey-blue tail

Pale yellow underside

COAL TIT

Grey-brown tit with no yellow, green, or blue on body, unlike Great or Blue tits; striking head pattern. Carries nuts away from feeders to eat nearby.

↔ 11.5cm

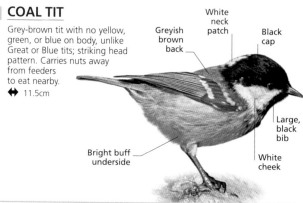

White neck patch

Greyish brown back

Black cap

Large, black bib

White cheek

Bright buff underside

LONG-TAILED TIT

Tiny-beaked bird with plump, round body and long, thin tail. Small flocks fly in single files between bushes. Low purr and sharp, whistled calls.

↔ 14cm

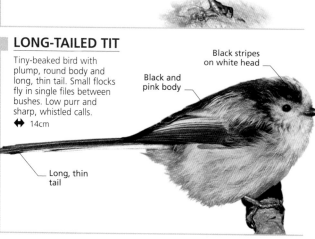

Black stripes on white head

Black and pink body

Long, thin tail

MARSH TIT

Plain brown, buff, and black tit with no green, yellow, or blue on body. Often seen in woods and bushes; scarce on feeders. Loud *pit-chew!* call.

↔ 11.5cm

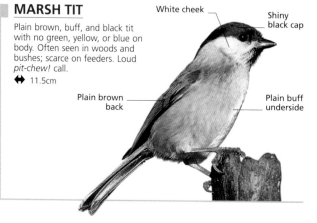

White cheek

Shiny black cap

Plain brown back

Plain buff underside

Pigeons & Doves

These are medium to large birds with soft plumage, rounded heads, and short legs and beaks. They are at home in trees and bushes or on the ground.

What to look out for • Head and neck pattern • Wing patterns • Tail patterns above and below • Size (Woodpigeon the biggest)

TOWN PIGEON

Familiar town-square bird, the "racing pigeon" gone wild. Varies in colour. Descended from Rock Dove, which still occurs in parts of northwest Europe, nesting on cliffs.

↔ 31–35cm

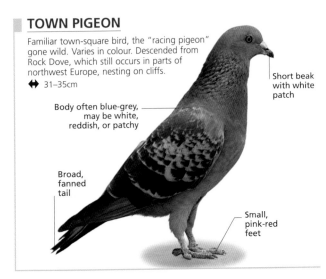

Short beak with white patch

Body often blue-grey, may be white, reddish, or patchy

Broad, fanned tail

Small, pink-red feet

WOODPIGEON

The biggest pigeon, with the longest wings and tail. Clatters loudly when taking flight. Sings soft *coo-coooo-coo-cu-cooo* song.

↔ 40–42cm

Big, white patch on neck

Pink chest

White patch on wing

Black and pale grey bands on tail

White on wing

STOCK DOVE

A small woodland or parkland pigeon with no white on wings or neck. Not a town bird, often found on fields with Woodpigeons.

↔ 32–34cm

Round, blue-grey head

Dark-edged wings with pale grey centre

Two short, dark bars on wing

No white on wing

COLLARED DOVE

A common dove, seen year-round. Slender, long-tailed, and very pale in colour. Sings three-note *cu-cooo-cuk* song; nasal *whurrr* call in flight.

↔ 31–33cm

Pinkish, sandy grey body and wings

Black collar

Slim, elongated shape

Tail black beneath with white tip

TURTLE DOVE

The smallest, most delicate dove; seen from April to September. Found in woods, hedges, and thickets; not a garden bird. Makes long, purring *coo*.

↔ 26–28cm

Striped neck patch

Chequered back

Pink breast

Black tail with white tip

Birds of Summer Skies

These are aerial feeders that catch insects over fields (Swallow), houses (House Martin), or water (Sand Martin). The Swift feeds over any habitat.

SWALLOW

Lithe, elegant summer visitor, with distinctive long, forked tail and dark throat. Seen in the air or perched on wires or TV aerials; often nests in or on buildings. Makes distinct, liquid *swit-swit-swit* call.

↔ 17–19cm

Shiny dark blue above

Long, forked tail

Pink- or buff-tinged underside

White spots across base of spread tail

HOUSE MARTIN

Small, aerial bird with characteristic white rump and underside. Builds mud nests under the eaves of buildings, or, more rarely, on cliffs.

↔ 12cm

Blue-black cap

Shiny, blue-black back

White rump above tail

White underneath, from chin to tail

Tiny, white-feathered legs and feet

What to look out for • Behaviour – perched or flying • Tail fork shape and length • Throat colour • Back and rump colour

SAND MARTIN

Tiny, aerial bird with distinctive, brown breastband. Makes long tunnels into earth or soft sandstone to nest. Often flies over water.

⬌ 12cm

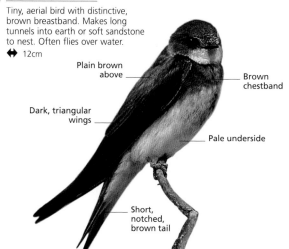

Plain brown above

Brown chestband

Dark, triangular wings

Pale underside

Short, notched, brown tail

SWIFT

Long-winged and fork-tailed; minute legs and feet. Always in the air, except when at its nest, hidden in a cavity in a building or a cliff. Makes loud, screeching calls.

⬌ 16–17cm

Dull pale chin

Brown-black all over

Long, scythe-like wings

SPARROWHAWK
P.54

CHAFFINCH
P.21

Tree canopy

The highest twigs and branches of trees form a woodland "canopy". In some woods, the canopy is open; in others, such as beech woods, it is closed and lets little light in. A number of birds live in this habitat, including Chaffinches, Blue Tits, and Redpolls.

BLUE TIT
P.26

JAY
P.40

2 WOODLAND & FOREST

Forests are home to a mixture of insect- and seed-eating birds. These include woodland specialists such as woodpeckers, Nuthatches, and Treecreepers, which stay in the trees, as well as others such as pigeons, tits, and thrushes, which also feed outside the wood.

TREECREEPER
P.39

GREAT SPOTTED WOODPECKER
P.38

Bark

Large branches and tree trunks are home to insects, insect larvae, spiders, and other invertebrates, which provide food for woodpeckers and Treecreepers. Trees also offer good nest sites for birds that nest in cavities.

GOLDCREST
P.35

WILLOW WARBLER
P.34

Understorey

Mid-height branches, shrubs, and saplings provide dense cover and good feeding opportunities for birds such as Blackcaps, warblers, Goldcrests, and Blackbirds. Many birds also use the forest floor to feed or nest.

BLACKCAP
P.34

Small Woodland Birds

These birds of woodland, shrubs, and parkland are sometimes also found in gardens. Only the Chiffchaff, Blackcap, and Goldcrest are seen in the UK during winter.

CHIFFCHAFF

Small warbler, similar to Willow Warbler, but more drab, with an olive look and darker legs. *Chiff-chaff-chiff-chaff* song.

↔ 10–11cm

Plain olive back

Pale half-circle under eye

Bobs tail frequently

Dark legs

WILLOW WARBLER

A warbler of low woods and trees near heaths and moors. Paler and sleeker than Chiffchaff, with a sweet, warbling song.

↔ 11cm

Pale greenish back

Long wingtips

Creamy yellow underneath

Pale legs

BLACKCAP

A warbler of woods and thickets; sometimes seen in big gardens in winter. Female has brown cap. Hard *tak* calls; song rich, fast, and warbling.

↔ 13cm

Black cap

Pale chin and throat

Grey underside

Brown wings

What to look out for • Leg colour • Tail colour • Head pattern • Presence of bars on wings

NIGHTINGALE

Plain, pale, red-brown bird of dense woods and low bushes. Famous for its song but secretive and shy.

↔ 16–17cm

Brown back

Pale ring and dark eye

Rusty red tail

REDSTART

Small, slender, Robin-like bird of woodland and nearby open spaces. Elusive in trees, but drops to the ground to feed, chasing insects with fluttering wings.

↔ 14cm

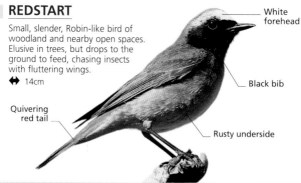

White forehead

Black bib

Quivering red tail

Rusty underside

GOLDCREST

Europe's smallest bird. Pale greenish in colour, with banded wings and plain face with striped crown that is visible close up. Often seen in conifers.

↔ 8.5–9cm

Yellow stripe on black crown

Broad white bar on wing

Pale body

Whitish face

Finches & Flycatchers

These small birds are commonly seen in forest clearings and parks (Spotted Flycatcher), and treetops (Pied Flycatcher, Crossbill, and Redpoll).

What to look out for • Head pattern and colour • Bars or flashes on wings • Streaks on upperparts and underside • Chin colour

CROSSBILL

A stocky finch of conifer woods; eats conifer seeds, also some berries, buds, and insects. Seen on treetops, but often comes down to drink from puddles. Loud, jarring *jip jip jip* calls.

↔ 16cm

Slightly pointed head

Hooked beak

Orange or red body

Red rump

REDPOLL ♀

Small, slim, streaked finch. Female has red cap and black bib; male also has red chest. Often seen with Siskin (p.20) in noisy, mixed flocks around birch and alder trees.

↔ 11–14.5cm

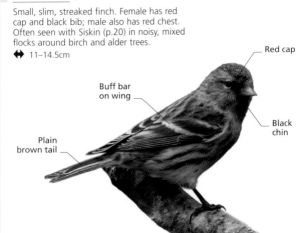

Red cap

Buff bar on wing

Black chin

Plain brown tail

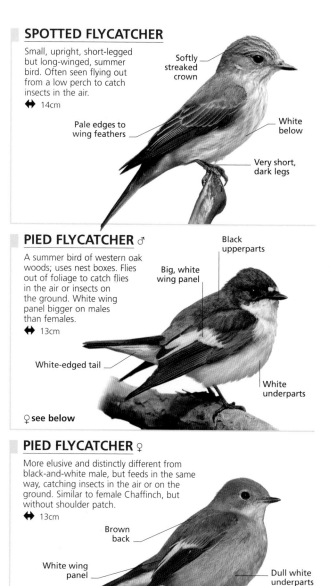

SPOTTED FLYCATCHER

Small, upright, short-legged but long-winged, summer bird. Often seen flying out from a low perch to catch insects in the air.
↔ 14cm

Softly streaked crown

Pale edges to wing feathers

White below

Very short, dark legs

PIED FLYCATCHER ♂

A summer bird of western oak woods; uses nest boxes. Flies out of foliage to catch flies in the air or insects on the ground. White wing panel bigger on males than females.
↔ 13cm

Black upperparts

Big, white wing panel

White-edged tail

White underparts

♀ see below

PIED FLYCATCHER ♀

More elusive and distinctly different from black-and-white male, but feeds in the same way, catching insects in the air or on the ground. Similar to female Chaffinch, but without shoulder patch.
↔ 13cm

Brown back

White wing panel

Dull white underparts

Short, dark legs

♂ see above

Bark Creepers

Woodpeckers cling to upright trunks and branches,
Treecreepers creep up or cling beneath branches, and
Nuthatches move freely in any direction.

What to look out for • Tail length and shape • Head
pattern • Beak shape • Colour on
rump and under tail

BLACK WOODPECKER

The biggest woodpecker.
Similar to a slim Jackdaw
(p.47) but with a red cap.
Perches upright against tree
trunks. Fast and direct flight.
A continental European bird,
not seen in the UK.

✦ 40–46cm

Red on
crown or
nape

Black body

Stiff black tail used as prop

GREAT SPOTTED WOODPECKER

A stunning, boldly patterned
bird. Often seen at garden
feeders. Known for its short,
vibrant, spring "drumming" –
made by hammering its beak
against a tree. Loud *tchik!* call.

✦ 22–23cm

Red patch
on head
(not present
on female)

Dagger-
like beak

Big, oval,
white
shoulder
patch

Bright red
under tail

Stiff tail used
as prop

GREEN WOODPECKER

Large, long woodpecker, with laughing call. Typical woodpecker flight pattern – deep, undulating action, then final, upward swoop to a perch.
↔ 30–33cm

Black around eye

Red crown

Green back

Yellow rump

TREECREEPER

Always seen creeping on tree bark. Looks like a mouse as it climbs up a branch before flying down to start again on another one.
↔ 12.5cm

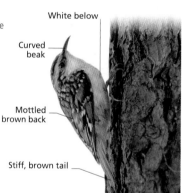

White below

Curved beak

Mottled brown back

Stiff, brown tail

NUTHATCH

This is a lively, active bird, common in woods and large gardens; often at feeders. Climbs without using its tail as a "prop" in the way that woodpeckers and treecreepers do.
↔ 12.5cm

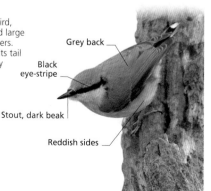

Grey back

Black eye-stripe

Stout, dark beak

Reddish sides

Other Woodland Birds

The Jay is a woodland crow, the Hoopoe is a dazzling bird of open ground, the Cuckoo is heard more than seen, and the Tawny Owl is a nocturnal bird of woods and gardens.

JAY

A shy crow of woodlands, but can also be seen in parks. Collects acorns in autumn, then buries them to eat when food is scarce. Big, white rump is noticeable in flight. Often detected by its raucous, rasping call.

↔ 34–35cm

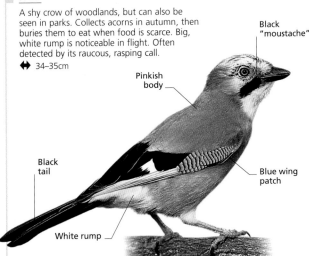

Black "moustache"

Pinkish body

Black tail

White rump

Blue wing patch

HOOPOE

This is a strikingly patterned bird, rarely seen in the UK. It can be elusive as it walks on the ground in dappled light and shade. Found in warm and dry grassy or sandy places.

↔ 26–28cm

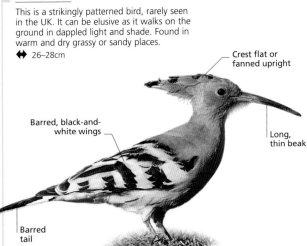

Crest flat or fanned upright

Barred, black-and-white wings

Long, thin beak

Barred tail

What to look out for • Head shape and pattern • Back colour
• Tail shape and pattern

CUCKOO

A large, grey bird, with a spotted tail and
drooping wings. More often heard than seen,
but easy to find by following *cuc-ooo* song.
Lays eggs in other birds' nests.

↔ 32–34cm

Grey back

Barred
underside

Very short,
orange legs

Dark tail
with white
spots

TAWNY OWL

Big-headed, with dark eyes.
Often seen in gardens and
parks. Makes hooting calls,
but also loud *ke-wick* notes
after dark.

↔ 37–39cm

Large,
round head

Black eyes

Row of
white spots
on shoulder

Short,
barred tail

3 OPEN COUNTRY

Modern farming methods mean fewer opportunities for birds, as they make fewer seeds and insects available. However, grassland, hedgerows, meadows, and less intensively cultivated fields all offer productive habitats for a variety of birds.

PHEASANT
Male, p.44

SKYLARK
P.49

JACKDAW
P.47

Open meadow

Grassland birds include the Grey Partridge, Jackdaw, Skylark, and Starling, which feed on insects, seeds, and worms at different times of year. Most feed their chicks high-nutrient insect food.

GREY PARTRIDGE
P.45

Skies

The open air should not be neglected as a habitat – Swifts and Swallows feed exclusively in the air, often over open farmland or moors, and Buzzards and Kestrels use the sky as an extra-high "perch" from which to see prey.

BUZZARD
P.56

Hedgerow

Some hedges have an abundance of berries, which are ideal for birds to eat in late summer, autumn, and early winter. Hedges are also great places for nesting for birds such as Rooks, Robins, Chaffinches, and Blackbirds.

ROOK
P.46

CHAFFINCH
P.21

BLACKBIRD
Male, p.24

YELLOWHAMMER
P.52

Gamebirds

These round-bodied, short-beaked birds are all chicken-like in general size and shape. They live in woods, fields and open spaces, and heather moors.

What to look out for • Tail length and shape • Plain or streaked back • Face colour and pattern • Tail colour in flight

PHEASANT ♂

A common bird released into wooded countryside and farmland in very large numbers for shooting. Many have white collars. Loud, crowing calls and sudden "whirr" of wings.

↔ 52–90cm

Red face

Green-black head

Rusty or coppery body with black spots

Very long, barred tail

♀ see below

PHEASANT ♀

Bigger than partridge and longer-tailed; shaped like the male but much less boldly coloured. Often seen at woodland edges.

↔ 52–90cm

Plain, pale brown head

Pale brown back with small black spots

Longer legs than partridge or grouse

Pointed, barred tail

♂ see above

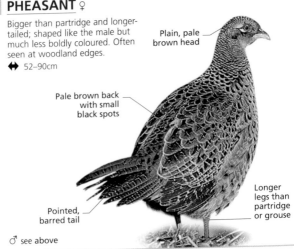

RED-LEGGED PARTRIDGE

Pretty, rounded partridge with striking patterns, especially on the head. Common in Spain, introduced in other places. Loud, curiously mechanical, repetitive "chucking" calls.

↔ 32–34cm

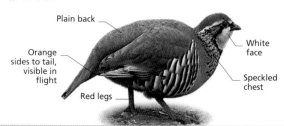

Plain back

Orange sides to tail, visible in flight

Red legs

White face

Speckled chest

GREY PARTRIDGE

Less common than it used to be in farmland and open country. Small, streaked partridge, much more subtle in colour than Red-legged Partridge. Male's call a creaky-gate" *kee-vick*.

↔ 29–31cm

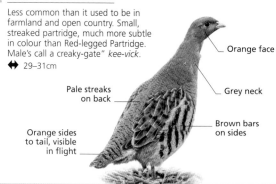

Pale streaks on back

Orange sides to tail, visible in flight

Orange face

Grey neck

Brown bars on sides

RED GROUSE

Bird of heather moors. Overall very dark red-brown. Secretive, but bursts into flight if disturbed; loud, staccato *kooo-rr-rr-or or-or go bak bak bak* calls.

↔ 40cm

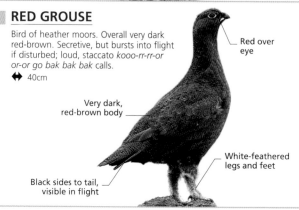

Very dark, red-brown body

Red over eye

White-feathered legs and feet

Black sides to tail, visible in flight

Crows

These thick-beaked and stout-legged birds are black or mostly black, and gather in groups. They are seen in open country, parks, and woodlands.

What to look out for • Tail length and shape • Shape and colour of beak, forehead, and face • Grey on neck or body

CARRION CROW

A big, black crow, much smoother-feathered than Rook and smaller and squarer-tailed than Raven. Found on open areas and in woodlands. Loud *caw* call.

↔ 44–51cm

Thick, pointed, black beak

Black body

Glossy plumage

Tightly feathered underside

ROOK

Big crow, with looser underside feathering, a much steeper forehead, and a sharper beak than Carrion Crow. Flies well, like a small Raven. Nests in treetop colonies.

↔ 44–46cm

Black body, with blue and purple tones

Bare white skin around base of beak

Longer, rounder tail than Carrion Crow

Loose, "baggy trousers" effect underneath

HOODED CROW

A grey-and-black version of the common Carrion Crow. Replaces Carrion Crow in places, including Scotland, the Isle of Man, Ireland, and parts of mainland Europe.

↔ 44–51cm

Black head and chest

Shape like Carrion Crow

Grey body

Black wings and tail

JACKDAW

Small, pigeon-like crow. Appears black but is actually mostly dark grey. Often mixes with Rooks on fields and in woodlands; also seen on old buildings.

↔ 33–34cm

Pale grey on back of neck

Black cap

Dark grey wings, with dull purple sheen in good light

Whitish eye

RAVEN

The world's biggest crow. Black body, like a giant Rook, with long wings and a rounded or diamond-shaped tail. Makes loud, echoing, throaty *crruk-crruk* and honking sounds.

↔ 56–57cm

Black plumage

Long, wedge-shaped tail

Throat feathers smoothed flat or raised in "beard"

Larks & Pipits

These are streaked, ground-loving birds. Larks are thicker-beaked and stockier than pipits. The Crested Lark is a continental European species not found in the UK.

MEADOW PIPIT

Slim, nervous bird, seen all year round. Smaller than a lark. Walks on the ground; *seep seep seep* flight calls. Pipits sing in the air, dropping like a shuttlecock with raised wings and tails.

↔ 14.5cm

Soft streaks on brown back

Slender, pointed beak

Black streaks on cream underside

Pale legs with long hind claws

TREE PIPIT

A summer bird. Similar to Meadow Pipit, but stockier and paler beneath. Streaks thick on breast but finer on sides. "Shuttlecock" flight like Meadow Pipit, finishing on a tree or a bush.

↔ 15cm

Pale line over eye

Black streaks on chest

Thin streaks on sides

Pale legs, with shorter hind claws than Meadow Pipit

ROCK PIPIT

Seaside equivalent of Meadow Pipit, but darker and greyer; yellower underneath with smudgier streaks. Flight call a slurred *tseep*.

↔ 16.5cm

Greyish back with soft streaks

Wide dark streaks on yellow-buff underside

Dark legs

Grey edge to tail

What to look out for • Head shape, especially presence of crest • Upperwing colour in flight • Tail colour • Leg colour of pipits

SKYLARK

Smallish ground bird, bigger than pipit. Walks and rarely perches above ground, unlike Corn Bunting (p.52), which hops and perches on wires. Continuous song from high, hovering flight.

↔ 18–19cm

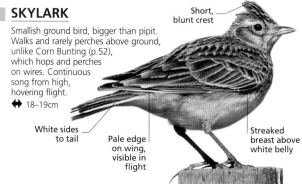

Short, blunt crest

White sides to tail

Pale edge on wing, visible in flight

Streaked breast above white belly

CRESTED LARK

Often seen on cornfields or waste ground. Looks orange-buff as it flies up; very short-tailed. Listen for loud, fluty *tree-loo-ee* calls.

↔ 17–19cm

Sharp, upright crest

Sharp streaks on chest

Sandy brown back

Wings plain orange-buff underneath

WOODLARK

A scarce lark of heathland and scattered trees. More boldly patterned than Skylark. Beautiful, repetitive song from a circling flight or high perch.

↔ 15cm

Long eye-stripe to back of neck

Dark cheek patch

White-black-white patch on edge of wing

Whitish corners to tail

Chats & Warblers

Chats are found in open or bushy country, the warblers in low, tangled thickets, bushes, and hedges. Only the Stonechat remains in Europe all year round.

WHEATEAR

Has big white patch above tail, obvious as it flies to a new, low perch. Keeps mostly to the ground on heaths, moors, and in grassy places.

↔ 14.5–15.5cm

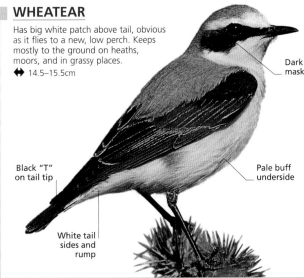

Dark mask

Pale buff underside

Black "T" on tail tip

White tail sides and rump

STONECHAT

Small bird of bushes, heaths, and coastal locations. Drops briefly to the ground to feed, but does not hop or run. Nervous *wheet-tac tac* calls.

↔ 12.5cm

Black head and throat

White wing patch

White neck patch

Reddish breast

What to look out for • Head shape • Wing colour and pattern • Rump and tail colour and pattern • Chin and throat colour

WHITETHROAT

A small, slender, bright warbler with long tail. Likes thick undergrowth and hedges. Scolding, churring calls.

✦ 14cm

Grey head

Reddish wings

Long tail with white sides

White throat and pinkish breast

SUBALPINE WARBLER

A small, pale bluish and pink warbler with slightly pointed head and longish tail. Found in dry, bushy places. A south European species, not seen in the UK.

✦ 12–13cm

Blue-grey above

White stripe below cheek

White-edged tail

Pink throat

Streaked Brown Birds

These triangular-beaked, seed-eating birds are found in open country; the Reed Bunting also inhabits wetlands. They all roam widely in countryside year-round.

CORN BUNTING

Stocky and big-billed. Similar to Skylark, but with plain wings and tail. Likely to perch on overhead wires or fenceposts. Song sounds like a bunch of keys being shaken.

↔ 18cm

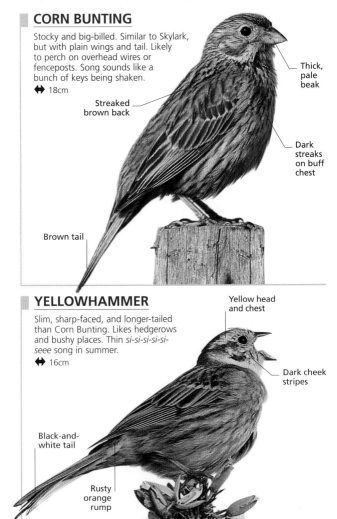

Thick, pale beak

Streaked brown back

Dark streaks on buff chest

Brown tail

YELLOWHAMMER

Slim, sharp-faced, and longer-tailed than Corn Bunting. Likes hedgerows and bushy places. Thin *si-si-si-si-si-seee* song in summer.

↔ 16cm

Yellow head and chest

Dark cheek stripes

Black-and-white tail

Rusty orange rump

What to look out for • Colour and pattern of head and chest
• Pattern of tail – white sides or flashes • Plain wings, or white-
streaked in flight • Rump colour (reddest on Yellowhammer)

REED BUNTING ♂

Dark and streaked. Found in low thickets
and damp places, mostly along watersides;
also visits gardens. Female is paler. Simple,
unmusical, jingling song.
↔ 15cm

Black beak
and head

White
collar

Black, brown, and
cream streaks
on back

Black-and-
white tail

♀ p.88

LINNET

Small, bouncy, lively finch. Found in
small flocks in bushy heathland or
on waste ground with low weeds.
Light, twittering calls.
↔ 12.5–14cm

Grey head
with red cap

Plain, ginger-
brown back

Red patches
on chest

White streaks
on wings
and tail

Small Birds of Prey

Among the varied birds of prey in Britain and Europe are sharp-winged falcons (Kestrel, Peregrine, Hobby), a blunt-winged hawk (Sparrowhawk), and two harriers.

KESTREL

Small, common falcon of open countryside; not commonly found in gardens. Often perches on poles and wires. Sometimes hovers in one spot above the ground.

↔ 34–39cm

Grey head

Chestnut back with black spots

Streaked, cream breast

Grey tail with black band on male

SPARROWHAWK

Small hawk; a common predator of woodland and farmland. Often seen dashing through gardens to take its prey (small birds) by surprise. Does not hover like Kestrel.

↔ 28–40cm

Short, blunt wings

Grey-brown back (male is blue-grey)

Barred, grey underside

Long, slim tail

HOBBY

Small, elegant falcon seen from April to September. Likes flying in the open air, above low-lying valleys, lakes, and heaths. Catches insects in flight.

↔ 28–35cm

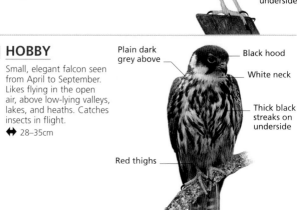

Plain dark grey above

Black hood

White neck

Thick black streaks on underside

Red thighs

What to look out for • Wing shape • Streaks or bars on underside • Head and cheek pattern, if any • Size and flight action

PEREGRINE

Large, broad-shouldered falcon of cliffs and large buildings. Catches pigeons and other birds in flight.

⬌ 39–50cm

Black hood and "moustache"

White neck and throat

Pale grey back

Grey bars on white underside

HEN HARRIER ♂

Large bird of prey. Flies low over heaths, moors, and marshes, gliding on raised wings. Female much browner than male.

⬌ 43–50cm

Grey head and body

Black wingtips

White rump

Long, slim legs

♀ p.57

MARSH HARRIER ♂

Large, broad-winged harrier of reed beds and wet places. Glides low on raised wings, but sometimes soars higher like Buzzard (p.56).

⬌ 48–55cm

Dark brown back

Black wingtips

Grey tail

Pale grey wing patch

♀ p.57

Large Birds of Prey

This group of brown birds includes female harriers, one of the most common birds of prey (Buzzard), and two prized rarities (Red Kite and Osprey).

What to look out for • Tail colour and shape • Wing shape and flight action • Colour and pattern of rump and tail • Head pattern

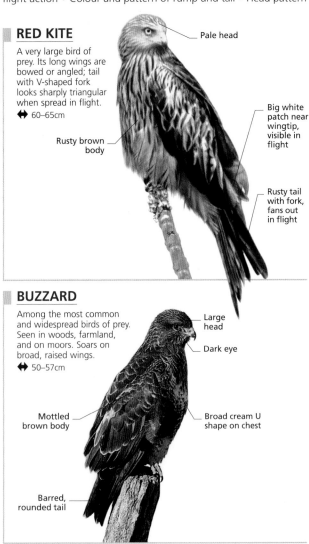

RED KITE

A very large bird of prey. Its long wings are bowed or angled; tail with V-shaped fork looks sharply triangular when spread in flight.

↔ 60–65cm

Pale head

Big white patch near wingtip, visible in flight

Rusty brown body

Rusty tail with fork, fans out in flight

BUZZARD

Among the most common and widespread birds of prey. Seen in woods, farmland, and on moors. Soars on broad, raised wings.

↔ 50–57cm

Large head

Dark eye

Mottled brown body

Broad cream U shape on chest

Barred, rounded tail

OSPREY

Rare bird of waterside woods and lakes; present from April to October. Often perches upright in big trees. Hovers over water and dives for fish.

↔ 52–60cm

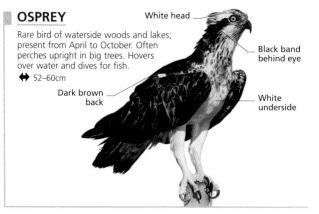

White head

Black band behind eye

Dark brown back

White underside

HEN HARRIER ♀

Large bird of moors, heaths, and marshy places. Glides with raised wings. Males and females look distinctly different – females are larger and broader-winged.

↔ 43–50cm

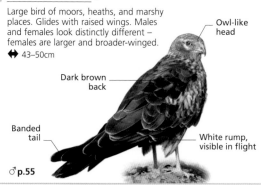

Owl-like head

Dark brown back

Banded tail

White rump, visible in flight

♂ p.55

MARSH HARRIER ♀

The largest, darkest harrier. Has creamy head and wing marks. Usually found hunting low over reeds.

↔ 48–55cm

Plain brown body

Cream cap and throat

Plain brown tail

♂ p.55

Birds of Prey

Birds of prey are large and impressive. They spend hours perched or soaring on warm air currents without using much energy. We see them most often in flight.

Identifying birds in flight can be difficult. It is hard to judge a bird's size against the sky, but looking at the flight action helps – is it light or heavy, fast or slow? Patterns, shapes, and postures are critically important because colours are difficult to make out on a flying bird.

What to look out for

• Look at wingtip shape: is it pointed, blunt, straight, or swept back?

• Is the tail closed or fanned, square or rounded, notched or forked?

• Does the head protrude or look squat? Is it broad or narrow?

• Do the wings have curved or straight sides?

• Is the flight action stiff and jerky or relaxed and "elastic"?

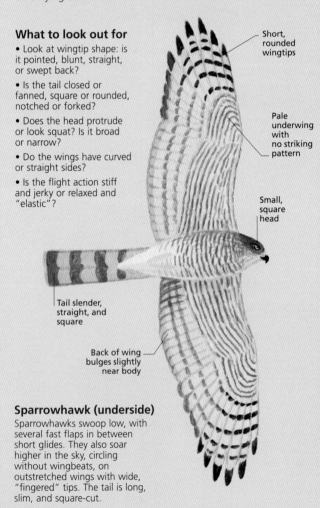

Short, rounded wingtips

Pale underwing with no striking pattern

Small, square head

Tail slender, straight, and square

Back of wing bulges slightly near body

Sparrowhawk (underside)

Sparrowhawks swoop low, with several fast flaps in between short glides. They also soar higher in the sky, circling without wingbeats, on outstretched wings with wide, "fingered" tips. The tail is long, slim, and square-cut.

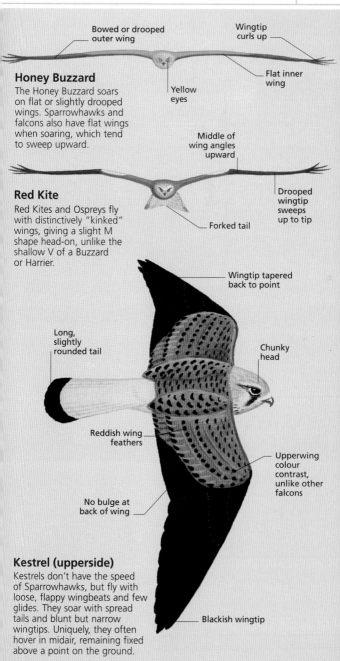

Honey Buzzard

The Honey Buzzard soars on flat or slightly drooped wings. Sparrowhawks and falcons also have flat wings when soaring, which tend to sweep upward.

Bowed or drooped outer wing

Wingtip curls up

Flat inner wing

Yellow eyes

Red Kite

Red Kites and Ospreys fly with distinctively "kinked" wings, giving a slight M shape head-on, unlike the shallow V of a Buzzard or Harrier.

Middle of wing angles upward

Drooped wingtip sweeps up to tip

Forked tail

Wingtip tapered back to point

Long, slightly rounded tail

Chunky head

Reddish wing feathers

Upperwing colour contrast, unlike other falcons

No bulge at back of wing

Blackish wingtip

Kestrel (upperside)

Kestrels don't have the speed of Sparrowhawks, but fly with loose, flappy wingbeats and few glides. They soar with spread tails and blunt but narrow wingtips. Uniquely, they often hover in midair, remaining fixed above a point on the ground.

SNIPE
P.80

LAPWING
P.78

Open shore

Wading birds such as the Snipe and Grey
Heron find food on or within mud, sand,
and silt, or in shallow water. Some birds
sieve water for seeds and minute animal
matter, while others probe the mud for
worms, or hunt fish and frogs.

GREY HERON
P.76

4 WATER &
WATERSIDE

Water adds great diversity
to the habitats and food in a
landscape, and so increases the
number and variety of birds. If
water is near woodland, swamp,
or open ground, the landscape
will be especially rich in wildlife.

KINGFISHER
P.88

GREAT CRESTED CREBE
P.72

MALLARD
Male, p.62

On the water
Some birds, such as the Coot, use open water as a safe refuge to sleep or rest. Others feed there, finding floating seeds and insects, or diving under water to find fish, shellfish, other invertebrates, or plants.

MOORHEN
P.73

Reeds and sedges
Many water birds, such as the Moorhen, are secretive and need dense vegetation to feed or nest in; others come to these areas to roost at night. Reedy areas alongside water are always worth a long, close look.

REED BUNTING
Female, p.88

REED WARBLER
P.86

Male Dabbling Ducks

These are surface-feeding (or dabbling) ducks that are at home on fresh water, salt water, and nearby marshes. The Mallard is common on ponds in parks.

■ MALLARD ♂

The most familiar park-pond duck, that comes easily for bread. Easily identified except in summer, when males are duller.
↔ 50–65cm

Glossy green head

Blue wing patch, edged white

Grey body with brown bands

♀ **p.64**

■ GADWALL ♂

A large duck; greyer than Mallard and best identified by white wing patch in flight. Mostly found on fresh water.
↔ 46–56cm

Pale, buff-grey head

Grey-brown body

Black rear body

Dark bill

♀ **p.64**

■ SHOVELER ♂

Large duck with big, broad beak; easy to identify by its bold colours. Found on freshwater and coastal marshes, but not on the open sea.
↔ 44–52cm

Green-black head

Long, broad-tipped, shovel-like bill

Reddish body

White breast

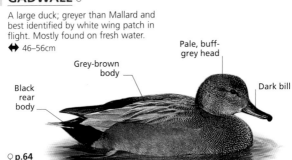

♀ **p.64**

What to look out for • Head colour • Colour patch or stripes on back of wing • Leg and bill colours – grey or orange • Colour patch under or beside tail

WIGEON ♂

Neat, very short-legged duck. Often gathers in dense flocks on water or grazes on nearby grass; occurs both inland and on the coast. Loud, explosive, whistling call.

↔ 45–51cm

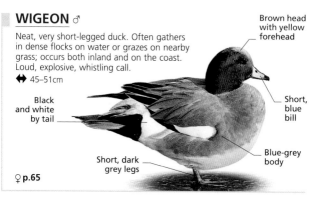

Brown head with yellow forehead

Short, blue bill

Blue-grey body

Black and white by tail

Short, dark grey legs

♀ **p.65**

TEAL ♂

The smallest duck. Although dark, its colours are visible at closer ranges in good light. Found inland and by the coast, often in muddy places.

↔ 34–38cm

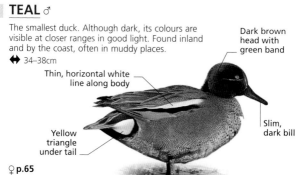

Dark brown head with green band

Thin, horizontal white line along body

Slim, dark bill

Yellow triangle under tail

♀ **p.65**

PINTAIL ♂

Large, elegant duck. Long tail may be harder to see than the bold colours. Found in salt marshes and wet places inland. Most common in autumn and winter.

↔ 53–70cm

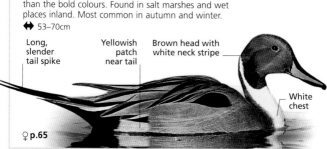

Long, slender tail spike

Yellowish patch near tail

Brown head with white neck stripe

White chest

♀ **p.65**

Female Dabbling Ducks

Male ducks are brightly coloured, but females are mostly brown. It is often possible to identify female ducks by the males they are accompanying.

MALLARD ♀

The biggest brown duck, with the loudest *quack quack quack* of all ducks. Has orange legs, and is common on park lakes and ponds.

↔ 50–65cm

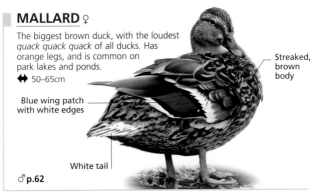

Streaked, brown body

Blue wing patch with white edges

White tail

♂ p.62

GADWALL ♀

Similar to Mallard but slightly smaller and neater. Has orange legs. White wing patch visible in flight. Usually seen on freshwater lakes and rivers.

↔ 46–56cm

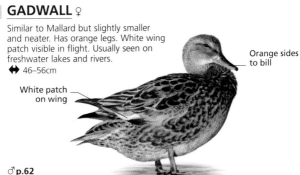

Orange sides to bill

White patch on wing

♂ p.62

SHOVELER ♀

Large duck with orange legs and a very broad beak, which is not so obvious at a distance. Dull blue shoulder patch visible in flight.

↔ 44–52cm

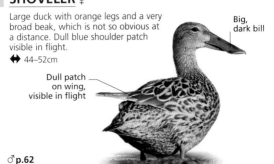

Big, dark bill

Dull patch on wing, visible in flight

♂ p.62

What to look out for • Colour patch or stripes on back of wing • Bill colours • Streaks or patches on or near tail • Bill size and shape

WIGEON ♀

A shy bird, forming tight flocks on water. Has grey legs. Often feeds in dense flocks on dry ground near water. Makes low growling noise, rather than a "quack".

↔ 45–51cm

Round, brown head

Short, grey bill

Mottled rather than streaked

♂ p.63

TEAL ♀

A tiny, grey-brown duck with dark legs and bill. Often found on muddy watersides or flying fast in small groups.

↔ 34–38cm

Bright green patch on wing

White streak beside tail

Dark, mottled body

♂ p.63

PINTAIL ♀

Looks like a slim, long-necked Mallard, but with darker beak, dark grey legs, and a more pointed tail.

↔ 53–70cm

Pale brown head and neck

Grey bill

Pointed tail

♂ p.63

Male Diving Ducks

Diving ducks feed under water, plunging beneath the surface of the water as they swim. Male diving ducks are colourful, strikingly patterned birds.

TUFTED DUCK ♂

A lively diving duck, commonly found on ponds, lakes, and reservoirs. Males can be identified by their distinctive, drooping crest and bold, piebald colour scheme.

✛ 40–47cm

Black head

Yellow eyes

Long tuft

Black body

White sides

Blue bill

♀ **p.68**

POCHARD ♂

Often seen with Tufted Duck, but greyer, with distinctive head colour and a grey wing stripe. Less active and feeds more at night.

✛ 42–49cm

Red-brown head

Pale grey back and sides

Dark from tail to rump

Black chest

♀ **p.68**

GOLDENEYE ♂

Widespread but less common than Tufted Duck. Very active; often dives almost non-stop for long periods, on both sea and inland waterways.

✛ 42–50cm

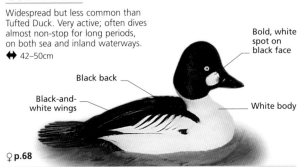

Bold, white spot on black face

Black back

Black-and-white wings

White body

♀ **p.68**

What to look out for • Head colour • Bill colour • White stripes, white patches, or grey bands on wing • Bill size and shape

GOOSANDER ♂

Large, long-bodied diving duck. Bigger than Red-breasted Merganser, with a simple but striking pattern. Found on freshwater lakes and rivers.

↔ 57–69cm

Hooked, dark red bill

Green-black head

Black back

White body

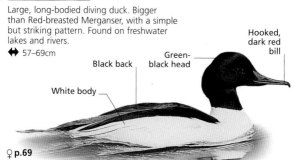

♀ p.69

RED-BREASTED MERGANSER ♂

A long-bodied diving duck. Similar to Goosander but with a more varied colour scheme and a more striking, spiky crest. Found on rivers, coasts, and large, sandy bays.

↔ 51–62cm

Blackish head with "double" spiky crest

Long, bright red bill

Grey body with white stripe on side

Dark chest

♀ p.69

EIDER ♂

Very large, heavy duck. Black-and-white in summer. Easily identified by its wedge-shaped head and beak. Found on sea coast and bays.

↔ 50–71cm

White head with black and green patches

Heavy, wedge-shaped bill

Black-and-white wings

Black underside

♀ p.69

Female Diving Ducks

Female diving ducks are plain in comparison to
their male counterparts, with predominantly brown
and grey bodies.

TUFTED DUCK ♀

Common freshwater diving duck. Mostly
dark brown, with yellow eyes and a small
"bump" on the back of its head. White
stripe visible on open wing.

✦ 40–47cm

Grey
bill with
black tip

Small tuft

♂ **p.66**

POCHARD ♀

Grey-brown diving duck. Often gathers in
mixed flocks with Tufted Ducks on freshwater
lakes. Flocks are tightly packed, often made
up largely of one sex.

✦ 42–49cm

Whitish ring
around eye

Long
tapered bill

Barred, grey-
brown back

Grey band
along spread
wing, visible
in flight

♂ **p.66**

GOLDENEYE ♀

Small, dark, rounded duck with a grey
body and a dark brown head. Summer
males look similar to females.

✦ 42–50cm

Dark brown
head

Short,
triangular
bill

White patches
on wing

♂ **p.66**

What to look out for • Head colour • Bill colour – grey, orange, or red • Bill shape and size • White stripes, white patches, or grey bands on wing

GOOSANDER ♀

A bigger, more sharply patterned bird than the similar Red-breasted Merganser. Shy, easily frightened bird.

↔ 57–69cm

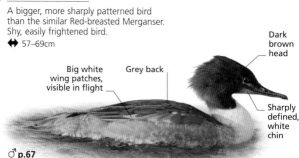

Dark brown head

Grey back

Big white wing patches, visible in flight

Sharply defined, white chin

♂ p.67

RED-BREASTED MERGANSER ♀

Browner plumage and a more smudged head and neck pattern than Goosander. Summer males and juveniles also have brown heads.

↔ 51–62cm

Wispy crest

Ginger-brown head

Brownish grey body

Slim, bright red bill

♂ p.67

EIDER ♀

A big, dark brown duck that is barred crosswise, rather than streaked lengthwise. Restricted to the sea, but often seen around coastal rocks and bays.

↔ 50–71cm

Wedge-shaped head

Barred body

Short tail, often raised

♂ p.67

Ducks

Duck plumage varies depending on age, sex, and season. Breeding male, summer male, female, and juvenile birds can look quite different.

Duck breeding plumages are at their best through winter and spring, when ducks pair up to mate. After that, males moult to a dull eclipse plumage for the summer – at this time of year camouflage is more important than splendid colour.

Mallards

Even the common, tame Mallards of park lakes are worth studying closely. Although males and females share a basic size and shape, they look different, and the male plumage changes with the seasons.

White tail

Blue wing patch

Dark olive beak

Curly tail

Female

Mallard females are brown all year round but can be identified by features such as the bright blue wing patch (speculum), white tail, and leg and bill colours.

Eiders

These ducks have a big, heavy appearance, with wedge-shaped heads and bills. You will only see them at the sea coast. The immature and female Eiders look very similar.

Wedge-shaped head

Female

The female Eider has a barred brown body and a paler head than the summer male, with a long wedge of facial feathers beside the thick bill.

Barred flanks

Immature

Young Eiders look much like females – they are barred crosswise, not lengthwise like most female ducks.

Head turns red-brown but in-between stages are frequent

Yellow beak

Summer male

Males in eclipse plumage look similar to females, but have redder feathers and yellow beaks. This male is halfway between eclipse and full breeding colours.

Green head

Winter male

Bright male Mallards in breeding plumage can be seen from late autumn to early spring. Their feathers are glossy and immaculate.

Yellow beak

White collar

Summer male

In non-breeding plumage the male Eider is mostly black-brown, with some paler patches and a pale streak behind its eye.

Pale eye-stripe

White back and flank patch

Pinkish chest

Winter male

In breeding plumage the male Eider is an unmistakeably pristine white, salmon-pink, and green.

Duck-like Birds

These are water and waterside species that can be seen throughout the year. They include rails (Moorhen and Coot), grebes, and a goose-like duck (Shelduck).

What to look out for • Beak and facial shield colour • Tail and rear end shape and colour • White stripes or patches on wing

GREAT CRESTED GREBE

Specialized diving bird; swims and dives like a duck but is not related. Has lobed (not webbed) toes and a dagger-like beak. Often found on the sea as well as freshwater lakes and rivers.

↔ 46–51cm

Sharp, pink beak

Black crest

Wide chestnut ruff

Bright white chest

LITTLE GREBE

Small, round, and almost tailless grebe. Frequently dives under the water. Mostly found inland, on rivers and lakes of all kinds. Has a loud, whinnying trill in summer.

↔ 25–29cm

Reddish cheeks

Black back

Very short tail

White spot at base of beak

SHELDUCK

Strikingly white; visible at very long range.
More goose-like than other ducks. Often
walks across mudflats or swims on
coastal pools and estuaries.
↔ 58–65cm

Bright
red beak

White body

Brown band
around chest

Pink legs

COOT

Appears very round-backed on water.
On land, can be identified by its big,
clumsy feet. A bird of fresh water, also
feeds a lot on nearby open shores.
Often gathers in large flocks.
↔ 36–38cm

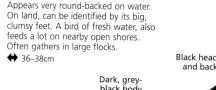
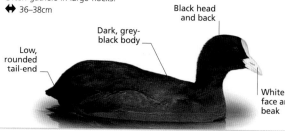

Black head
and back

Dark, grey-
black body

Low,
rounded
tail-end

White
face and
beak

MOORHEN

Common, fairly secretive bird of fresh
water and adjacent wet ground; creeps
or flutters away if disturbed. Found in
smaller groups than Coot.
↔ 32–35cm

Red and
yellow
beak

White
flash under
cocked tail

Green legs
and long,
slender toes

White stripe
along side

Geese

These large birds are often found on or near water and in open fields. They are mostly sociable and some form flocks of many thousands in autumn and winter.

What to look out for • Beak and leg colour • Head, neck, and chest pattern • Contrast and pattern of wings in flight • Behaviour and location

CANADA GOOSE

A big, brown goose; often rather tame. Found on park lakes and town riversides. Introduced from North America; present all year round. Particularly loud, honking call in flight.

↔ 90–110cm

Barred, brown body

White chinstrap

Black neck and head

Pale chest

GREYLAG GOOSE

A big, grey-brown goose with very pale grey wings. Has distinctly coloured beak and legs. Found in wild flocks in the winter and also in semi-tame flocks year round.

↔ 74–84cm

Orange beak

Pale brown head and neck

White around tail

Pink legs

PINK-FOOTED GOOSE

Smaller and darker than Greylag Goose.
Migrates from Iceland in large flocks.
Found on coastal fields and
marshes. Sharp *wink wink*
call in flight.
↔ 64–76cm

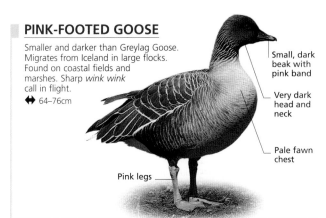

Small, dark
beak with
pink band

Very dark
head and
neck

Pale fawn
chest

Pink legs

BRENT GOOSE

The smallest and darkest goose. Found
along low-lying coasts with fields and
in estuaries. Often "upends" in salt
marsh creeks, tipping forward so its
head is under water, but tail is above.
↔ 56–61cm

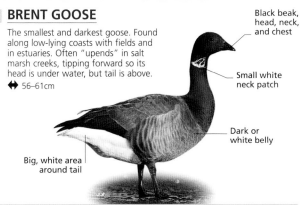

Black beak,
head, neck,
and chest

Small white
neck patch

Dark or
white belly

Big, white area
around tail

WHITE-FRONTED GOOSE

Best identified by its strong patterns and
brightly coloured legs. Found on grassy
meadows and marshes. Scarce in the
UK, but common in northwest
Europe during winter.
↔ 65–78cm

White flash
on forehead

Pink
beak

Black bars
on belly

Orange legs

Large Waterside Birds

The heron, egret, and stork are tall, leggy waterside birds. Of the three swans, the Whooper and Bewick's are winter birds in Europe and breed in the far north.

GREY HERON

A very large, upright bird. Large and broad-winged in flight, with its wings deeply arched, and its long neck coiled back into the shoulders.

↔ 90–98cm

Dark stripe through eye to wispy crest

Long, S-shaped neck

Black shoulder patch

Pale grey back and plumes

Black sides

LITTLE EGRET

Sparkling white heron, with "yellow slippers" on its long, black legs. Its numbers have increased almost everywhere, but it remains mainly close to the coast.

↔ 55–65cm

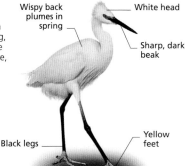

Wispy back plumes in spring

White head

Sharp, dark beak

Black legs

Yellow feet

WHITE STORK

Huge bird of southern and central Europe. Very flat wings in flight, unlike Grey Heron's. Arrives in Europe in early spring, leaves for Africa in autumn. Flies in large, soaring, circling flocks.

↔ 0.95–1.1m

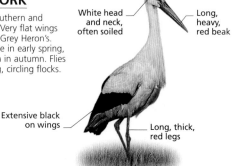

White head and neck, often soiled

Long, heavy, red beak

Extensive black on wings

Long, thick, red legs

What to look out for • Beak colour and pattern • Position of head and neck in flight • Tail shape and length • Colour of legs and feet

MUTE SWAN

The common swan that comes for bread on park lakes; also lives on large lakes, rivers, and along the sea coast. Powerful flight, with neck outstretched. Present all year in most places.
↔ 1.4–1.6m

Black and orange beak, with knob at base

Wings often arched

Slim, pointed tail, often raised

Beak usually held pointing downwards

WHOOPER SWAN

A large wild swan, found from autumn to spring in most of Europe. Gathers in groups, sometimes mixed with other swans. Some found inland, but most are seen close to the coast.
↔ 1.4–1.6m

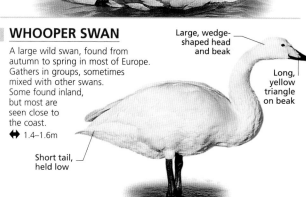

Large, wedge-shaped head and beak

Long, yellow triangle on beak

Short tail, held low

BEWICK'S SWAN

Smaller version of Whooper Swan, best identified by its beak pattern. Flocks with Mute Swan, Whooper Swan, or both. Often on fields and marshes inland from late autumn to spring.
↔ 1.15–1.27m

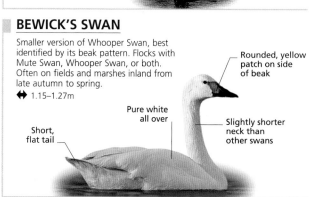

Rounded, yellow patch on side of beak

Pure white all over

Short, flat tail

Slightly shorter neck than other swans

Wading Birds

These are all waders, but the Lapwing and Golden Plover prefer waterside or dry ground. The Grey Plover is an estuary bird; the Black-winged Stilt likes shallow pools.

LAPWING

Large bird, with a wispy crest and wide, rounded wings. Looks black and white at long range, greener close up. Often gathers in flocks on marshes and open fields.

↔ 28–31cm

Black cap and crest

Glossy green back

Black chest patch

White belly

GOLDEN PLOVER

Often mixes with Lapwings, forming large flocks on fields and grassy marshlands. The two species separate in flight, as Golden Plovers are faster and sharper-winged than blunt-winged Lapwings.

↔ 26–29cm

Round head and small beak

Speckled, yellow and brown back

Pale face

White underwing, visible in flight

White underside in winter (black in summer)

What to look out for • Pattern beneath wing • Back colour and pattern • Head and face colour and shape • Beak size and shape

GREY PLOVER

Feeds mostly on mudflats and estuaries. Unlike Golden Plover, has black "armpits" and white rump, which are visible in flight. Less likely to mix with Lapwings and Golden Plovers; often seen with godwits, Curlews, and Redshanks.

↔ 27–30cm

Round head

Thick beak

Speckled grey and black above

Black face and underside in spring (dull white in winter)

Black underside and base of wing

BLACK-WINGED STILT

Found in much of Europe, but rare in the UK. Wades deeply in fresh or brackish water on extremely long legs. Loud, nervous, chattering calls.

↔ 33–36cm

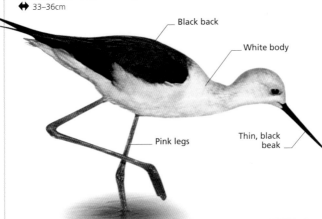

Black back

White body

Pink legs

Thin, black beak

Brown Waders

These waders are brownish, except for the striking Oystercatcher. The Snipe is restricted to fresh water, and the Common Sandpiper prefers fresh to salt water.

GREEN SANDPIPER

A smallish wading bird; dark except for its white belly. Appears more black-and-white in flight. Fluty, yodelling call.

↔ 21–24cm

Dark back with white specks

Pale stripe from beak to eye

Wing brown above, darker beneath

Pure white underneath

COMMON SANDPIPER

The brownest sandpiper, with a longer tail than most small wading birds. Bobs its head and swings its tail up and down while walking. Ringing *tswee-wee-wee* call.

↔ 19–21cm

Mid-brown above

Long, white wing stripe on brown wing, visible in flight

White "hook" in front of wing

Dull yellow-brown legs

SNIPE

A secretive bird of very wet, muddy places, as well as long grass or sedges. Flies up fast with a zigzag course. Call sounds like tearing cloth.

↔ 25–28cm

Striped back

Long, black and cream stripes on head

Short, rusty orange tail

Very long, straight beak

What to look out for • Wing and rump pattern in flight • Leg colour • Head and upperside pattern • Flight action and take-off behaviour – low or steep

OYSTERCATCHER

A big, black-and-white bird, easily identified by its striking appearance. Found on coasts, undisturbed fields, and riversides inland. Loud, piping calls.

↔ 40–45cm

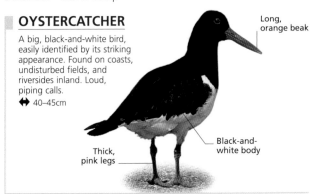

Long, orange beak

Black-and-white body

Thick, pink legs

GREENSHANK

A scarce wading bird. Bigger and more elegant than Redshank. Seen most often in autumn, in most places. Loud, even *chew-chew-chew* call.

↔ 30–35cm

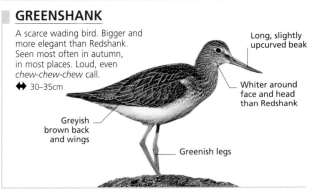

Long, slightly upcurved beak

Whiter around face and head than Redshank

Greyish brown back and wings

Greenish legs

REDSHANK

More common, smaller, browner, and usually noisier than Greenshank. Often found in large numbers on estuaries and wet areas inland. Ringing *tyew-yew-ew* call.

↔ 27–29cm

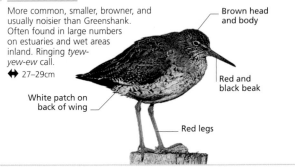

Brown head and body

Red and black beak

White patch on back of wing

Red legs

Coastal Waders

These waders tend to favour coastal habitats, but they can be seen inland on migration. Curlews and godwits are large, the others are smaller.

CURLEW

The largest wader. Gull-like in flight, but with longer legs. Looks plain and dark from a distance. Loud, beautiful *cur-lew* call; long, trilling song.

✤ 50–60cm

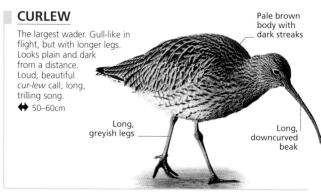

Pale brown body with dark streaks

Long, greyish legs

Long, downcurved beak

BLACK-TAILED GODWIT

A large wader, but much smaller than Curlew. Plainer and greyer than Bar-tailed Godwit in winter, with longer legs and a bolder pattern in flight.

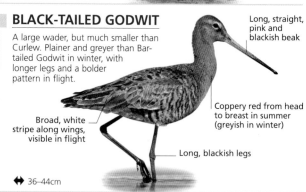

Long, straight, pink and blackish beak

Coppery red from head to breast in summer (greyish in winter)

Broad, white stripe along wings, visible in flight

Long, blackish legs

✤ 36–44cm

BAR-TAILED GODWIT

A big, streaky brown wader. Found on large sand and mud estuaries and wide, open beaches, unlike Black-tailed Godwit, which prefers sheltered creeks.

✤ 33–42cm

Brownish wings

Streaky brown head and back

Long, slightly upcurved beak

Dark, medium-length legs

What to look out for • Wing and rump pattern in flight
• Beak length and shape • Leg length and proportions above
and below the joint • Size – small, medium, large, or very large

DUNLIN

A common wading bird of muddy
beaches; also appears by inland lakes
in spring and autumn. Often in flocks.
Distinctive *shrree* or *treerrr* call.

↔ 16–20cm

Streaked, grey-
brown head and back
(brighter in summer)

Thin,
slightly
curved
beak

Streaked belly
(black in
summer)

Very dark legs

SANDERLING

A stockier, straighter-billed wader than
Dunlin, with black legs. Also, much
more restricted to open sandy or silty
shores than Dunlin. Runs very fast
beside the tideline.

↔ 20–21cm

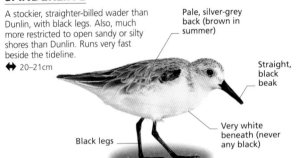

Pale, silver-grey
back (brown in
summer)

Straight,
black
beak

Very white
beneath (never
any black)

Black legs

KNOT

Between Dunlin and Redshank (p.81) in size;
medium-sized beak and legs. Plods rather
than runs. Often seen in large flocks that
fly with amazing coordination. Grey
patch above tail visible in flight.

↔ 23–27cm

Short,
straight
beak

Dull grey in winter

Grey-green legs

Small Waders

These similar-looking birds are found in different habitats: sea coasts (Turnstone), inland and on the coast (Ringed Plover), and by fresh water (Little Ringed Plover).

TURNSTONE

A smallish, stocky, thick-billed, orange-legged wading bird. Brightly coloured in spring, becomes darker in winter. Distinctive white wing and back patches visible in flight. Found on stony or rocky coasts, unlike other waders, which usually prefer soft ground such as sand or mud.
↔ 21–24cm

Black-and-white head pattern (more black-brown in winter)

White shoulder patches

Black, white, and orange back (more black and brown in winter)

Orange legs

LITTLE STINT

Tiny wader, smaller than a sparrow. In UK juveniles are most common during autumn migration, with occasional adults in spring. Has cream V shape on rusty back, which is most obvious from rear. Often seen with Dunlins (p.83) but can be told apart by its smaller size and whiter underside.
↔ 12–14cm

Pale stripe over dark ear patch

Black spots and buff scales above

White underside

What to look out for • Wing and rump pattern in flight • Leg colour • Pattern of head and upperside • Beak colour • Presence of eye-ring

RINGED PLOVER

Small, stocky waterside bird of salt- and freshwater coasts. Other "ringed" plovers have similarly patterned heads, but none in Europe have such a brightly coloured bill and legs. Call a liquid *tlu-ip!* note. White wing stripe visible in flight.
↔ 17–19cm

Black and white bands on head and chest

Orange-and-black beak

No streaks on brown back or white underside

Bright orange legs

LITTLE RINGED PLOVER

A small, sleek, "ringed" plover. Is only seen in Europe from spring to autumn, unlike Ringed Plover. Breeds at waterside or in dry, rough, open spaces. Makes a single, short *pew* note.
↔ 14–15cm

Yellow eye-ring

Plain wing (white stripe on Ringed Plover)

Black beak

Dull pinkish legs

Wetland Warblers

These are small birds of dense, waterside vegetation: reeds and willows (Reed Warbler), wet thickets (Sedge Warbler), and waterside thickets (Cetti's Warbler).

REED WARBLER

A summer bird. Plain brown above and buff beneath, with a whiter bib. Often found on reed beds; sometimes breeds in drier areas. Sings with a regular, repetitive, churring rhythm.

✦ 13–14cm

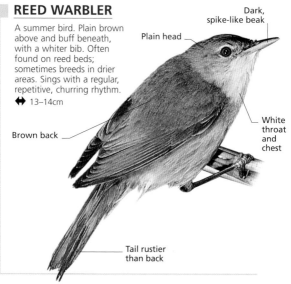

Dark, spike-like beak

Plain head

Brown back

White throat and chest

Tail rustier than back

GRASSHOPPER WARBLER

Heard more often than seen; high, metallic, reeling trill, which is too high-pitched for some people to hear. Sings from low bramble or bush overgrown with long grass, or creeps quietly through dense vegetation.

✦ 12.5cm

Softly streaked crown

Soft, spotted lines on olive-brown back

Unmarked, yellowish-buff underside

Longish, rounded tail

What to look out for • Streaked or plain back • Head pattern
• Neck and chest colour • Colour of rump and tail

SEDGE WARBLER

Best identified by its head pattern.
A summer bird; found in nettles
and bushy thickets by water more
often than Reed Warbler. Varied,
scolding, chattering song.
↔ 13cm

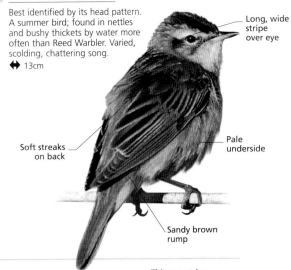

Long, wide
stripe
over eye

Pale
underside

Soft streaks
on back

Sandy brown
rump

CETTI'S WARBLER

Present all year round. A very
elusive, small, dark warbler of
deep, waterside bushes and
swamps. Best detected by its
sudden, abrupt, loud, liquid
burst of song.
↔ 14cm

Thin eye-stripe

Dark
head

Grey
sides of
neck and
chest

Dark,
red-brown
back and tail

Broad,
rounded
tail tip

Small Waterside Birds

These birds include three wagtails that like wet or damp places; the Kingfisher, which must have clean, open water; and the Reed Bunting, a wetland or marsh bird.

What to look out for • Back and rump colour • Leg colour • Underside colour

KINGFISHER

Upright, dumpy shape and a long beak. Unique for its headlong dives (with a loud *plop*) into water. Often heard calling a loud, sharp *keee*, before a blue flash is seen dashing along a stream.

↔ 16–17cm

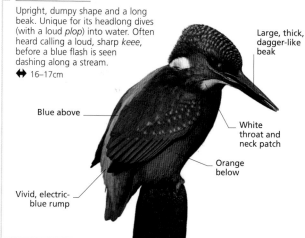

Blue above

Vivid, electric-blue rump

Large, thick, dagger-like beak

White throat and neck patch

Orange below

REED BUNTING ♀

A small, finch-like bird. Has a long, black-and-white tail, and its back is heavily streaked with black. Stays close to the waterside in dense vegetation. Calls are short and high-pitched.

↔ 15cm

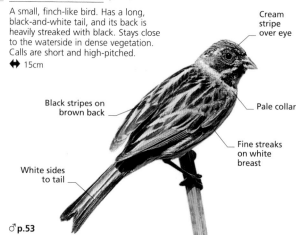

Black stripes on brown back

White sides to tail

Cream stripe over eye

Pale collar

Fine streaks on white breast

♂ p.53

PIED WAGTAIL

Small, with a long tail. Easily identified by its black, white, and grey patterns. Walks fast and flicks its tail. Found on open ground, including car parks and roadside paths.

◆ 18cm

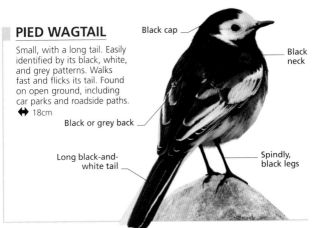

Black cap

Black neck

Black or grey back

Long black-and-white tail

Spindly, black legs

GREY WAGTAIL

Mostly grey and pale buffish in colour. Can be mistaken for Yellow Wagtail due to the yellow patch around the base of its tail. Present year-round, unlike Yellow Wagtail.

◆ 18–19cm

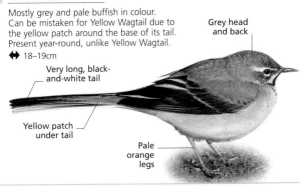

Grey head and back

Very long, black-and-white tail

Yellow patch under tail

Pale orange legs

YELLOW WAGTAIL

The yellowest wagtail, with spindly, black legs and the least obvious, least wagged tail. Seen in Europe from spring to autumn.

◆ 17cm

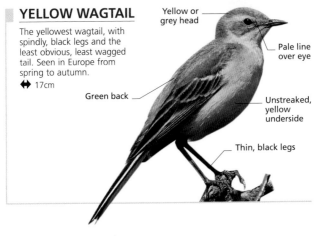

Yellow or grey head

Pale line over eye

Green back

Unstreaked, yellow underside

Thin, black legs

GUILLEMOT
P.100

SANDERLING
P.83

OYSTERCATCHER
P.81

Sheer cliffs

Cliffs provide secure nesting places for birds that live at sea, such as Guillemots and Kittiwakes. They also shelter nesting land birds such as Peregrines from disturbance and predators.

Sandy shore

Sand and shingle are easily swept or blown away, and make difficult places for tiny animals to live. This means that only a few birds feed on sandy shores, but many gulls, terns, and plovers nest on remote shingle banks.

5 COAST & SEA

Just as fresh water adds variety to the land, so the sea enriches any coastal habitat – even urban ones. Many birds can be seen from promenades and in coastal towns. The less disturbed areas of saltmarsh, estuary, and seacliff, however, are particularly rich in bird-life.

Estuaries

Occurring where rivers meet the sea, estuaries are a mix of fresh and salt water. They are rich and varied places; tides cover and expose mud and silt twice a day, bringing nutrients for the invertebrates that live there, and creating opportunities for birds to feed on them.

REDSHANK
P.81

GANNET
P.102

FULMAR
P.95

SHAG
P.102

At sea

Seabirds are wonderfully adapted to a
tough ocean life. They can be seen
flying past headlands, especially during
heavy winds, but to see them truly at
home in this demanding environment,
it is best to get out in a boat.

SHELDUCK
P.73

Muddy shore

The weighty stability of mud
and the rich nutrients brought in by
the tides mean that muddy shores,
creeks, and estuaries are much better
for most birds than sand. However,
at high tide, waders such as the Knot
need to find safe refuge elsewhere.

KNOT
P.83

Large Gulls

These common, noisy, and large water birds are mostly white and grey. They fly well, soaring high, and are good swimmers, but are just as at home on dry land.

HERRING GULL

The typical, noisy gull spotted on rooftops, promenades, and beaches. A bossy and aggressive bird; head turns grey-brown in winter. Pale eyes, unlike Common Gull (p.94).

↔ 55–67cm

Pale eye

Red spot on yellow beak

White head in summer

Pale grey back

Black wingtips with white spots

Pink legs

LESSER BLACK-BACKED GULL

As big as Herring Gull, but slimmer; much smaller than Great Black-backed Gull. Head smudged grey-brown in autumn–winter. Gathers in large flocks.

↔ 52–67cm

Head white in summer

Dark grey back

Slender, black-and-white wingtips

Yellow legs

What to look out for • Size – large or very large (Great Black-backed Gull) • Beak and leg colour, which may change with seasons • Wingtip patterns, especially on open wings • Back and wing colour, from pale grey to black

GREAT BLACK-BACKED GULL

The biggest gull; dramatic in flight and impressively well-built on the ground. Less common than other gulls, but very widespread.
↔ 64–78cm

White head

Yellow bill with red spot

Black back and wings

Pale pink legs

YELLOW-LEGGED GULL

Similar to Herring Gull, but with a slightly darker back, and a white head in winter as well as in summer. Mainly found in the Mediterranean region.
↔ 55–65cm

White head

Smooth, mid-grey back

Long, black-and-white wingtips

Yellow legs

Small Gulls & Fulmar

Gulls divide their time between sea and land, except the Kittiwake, which only comes to land to nest. The Fulmar looks like a gull, but is not related to them.

What to look out for • Back, rump, and tail colour • Beak and leg colour • Wingtip patterns, especially in flight • Head pattern

BLACK-HEADED GULL

Common, noisy, squabbling gull. Small, very pale, with broad, white flash on the front of open wings. Beak and legs deep red in summer, brighter in winter. White head with brown hood in summer.
↔ 34–37cm

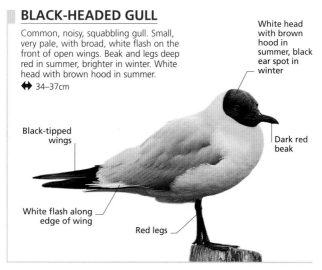

White head with brown hood in summer, black ear spot in winter

Black-tipped wings

Dark red beak

White flash along edge of wing

Red legs

COMMON GULL

Similar to small, dark Herring Gull (p.92), but with different leg and beak colours, and gentle, dark eye. Often found on grassy fields and muddy beaches.
↔ 38–44cm

Small, greenish yellow beak

Mid-grey back

Large, black-and-white wingtips

Green legs

MEDITERRANEAN GULL

A once scarce bird that is now increasing in number. Similar to Black-headed Gull but paler, with pure white underwing and pearly grey upperwing.

Jet-black hood in summer, white head with dark eye-patch in winter

Bright red beak

Unmarked white wingtips

Red or blackish legs

↔ 36–38cm

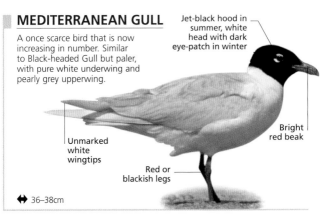

KITTIWAKE

Seagoing gull, seen on coastal cliffs but not inland. Similar to small, delicate Common Gull but has very short, black legs. Calls loud *kitti-a-wa-ake* from cliffs or ledges on coastal buildings.

↔ 38–40cm

Dark eye

Small, yellowish beak

Unmarked, black wingtips

Short, blackish legs

FULMAR

Gull-like seabird of cliffs and open seas, but not related to gulls. Cannot stand or walk due to weak legs, but is a very strong flier on stiff wings.

↔ 45–50cm

Big, white head

Large, dark eye

Stubby, hooked, grey-and-yellow beak

Patchy, grey wings

Grey tail

Gulls

Large gulls take several years to mature fully. As they get older their plumage changes, making it possible to tell the ages of different individuals.

Changes in plumage come about when birds moult – old feathers fall out and new ones grow. Gulls start off brown and become pale grey, white, and black with age. After four years, adult gulls alternate between breeding (summer) and non-breeding (winter) plumage – look for changes in spring and late summer/autumn. The birds shown here are all Herring Gulls.

Blackish beak

Sharp black wingtips with white spots

Dark bars on back

Black wingtips and tail band

First year

A gull's first feathers are its brownish juvenile plumage. In its first autumn, a gull moults into its first winter plumage. It moults again in spring into its first summer plumage. The beak remains almost black.

Yellow-and-black beak

Extensive grey on wings and back

White underparts

Third year

In the second and third years, all feathers change each autumn, and head and body feathers change again each spring, making the young gull look progressively more like an adult.

Summer adult

After four years, it is impossible to tell a Herring Gull's precise age by its plumage. However, breeding and non-breeding plumages alternate by season.
In summer, an adult gull has a pure white head and bright beak and leg colours.

Pale eye with orange ring

Bright yellow beak with red spot

Grey back and wings

White chest and head

Eye-ring less orange than in summer

Heavily streaked head and breast

Winter adult

In the winter, adult Herring Gulls have brown-streaked heads. The streaked head and breast return to white in spring.

Body same as in summer

Terns

Most terns are seabirds, but the Common Tern is equally at home inland. Terns are long-distance migrants – they fly south in autumn and return in spring.

COMMON TERN

A sleek, slender bird. Similar to Arctic Tern but paler, longer-legged, and with a more southerly distribution. Found on coasts, inland lakes, and rivers.

✦ 31–35cm

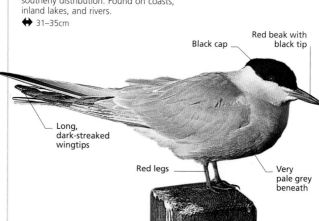

Black cap

Red beak with black tip

Long, dark-streaked wingtips

Red legs

Very pale grey beneath

ARCTIC TERN

More strictly a seabird than Common Tern, with shorter legs and a shorter, spikier beak. Outer wing translucent in flight. Nests on rocky islands. Migrates past southern coasts on its way to Southern Ocean in spring and autumn.

✦ 32–35cm

Red beak

Black cap

Grey back

Silvery grey wingtips

Mid-grey beneath

Red legs

What to look out for • Beak and leg colour and pattern
• Wingtip pattern in flight, above and below • Leg length

SANDWICH TERN

The largest among the most widespread
terns, and the palest. Often seen fishing
in sandy, coastal bays, diving in with a big
splash. Raucous *kier-ink* call.

↔ 36–41cm

Long, black
beak with
pale tip

Very pale, silvery
grey back

White
beneath

Black legs

LITTLE TERN

The tiniest tern. Usually seen on the
coast, flying fast and dashing into
the sea for small fish. Rare bird of
sand and shingle beaches.

↔ 22–24cm

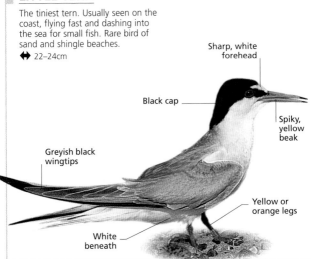

Sharp, white
forehead

Black cap

Spiky,
yellow
beak

Greyish black
wingtips

Yellow or
orange legs

White
beneath

Specialist Seabirds

Strictly seabirds, these auks rarely come to land, except to nest on cliffs. The Black Guillemot nests on rocky islets in more northerly locations.

▌ PUFFIN

Small, upright bird of coastal cliffs and islands, or the open sea. Nests in cavities high on cliffs. Scarce off headlands away from its nesting sites. Flies low and fast over the waves.
↔ 26–29cm

Triangular, multicoloured beak

Round head with grey cheeks

Black chestband and back

Orange legs

▌ GUILLEMOT

A slim, sharp-beaked seabird. Nests on ledges and on the tops of offshore rocks near the coast. Swims or flies fast and low over the sea.
↔ 38–54cm

Pointed, dagger-like beak

Dark brown back and wings

White belly

Short, square tail

What to look out for • Beak shape, colour, and pattern
• Leg colour • Presence of wing patch • Nesting site location

RAZORBILL

Stockier and thicker-billed than
Guillemot. Found on the open
sea or sea cliffs in summer. Nests
in cavities high on cliffs. Swims in
close flocks in larger estuaries.
↔ 37–39cm

Black head,
neck, and back

Thick,
hooked
beak
with white
lines

White
belly

Pointed,
black tail

BLACK GUILLEMOT

Smaller than Guillemot. Plumage is
mottled much whiter in winter than in
summer. Nests on low, rough boulders
in rocky islets and on cliffs. Seen around
coasts more often than Guillemot.
↔ 30–32cm

Smoky black
head and body

White wing
patch

Short,
pointed
beak

Short, red legs

Large Seabirds

In this group only the Cormorant goes inland, nesting on trees and coastal cliffs. The Gannet nests in dense colonies, and the Shag in smaller groups on the coast.

What to look out for • Face pattern, especially cheek and fleshy pouch by the beak

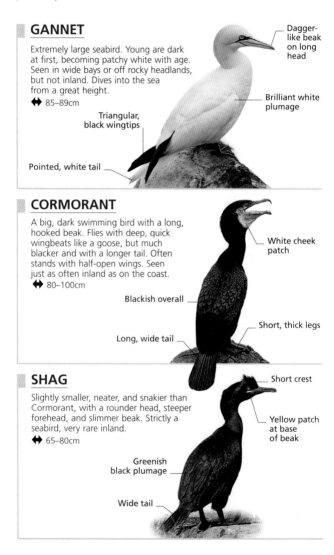

GANNET

Extremely large seabird. Young are dark at first, becoming patchy white with age. Seen in wide bays or off rocky headlands, but not inland. Dives into the sea from a great height.

⟷ 85–89cm

Triangular, black wingtips

Pointed, white tail

Dagger-like beak on long head

Brilliant white plumage

CORMORANT

A big, dark swimming bird with a long, hooked beak. Flies with deep, quick wingbeats like a goose, but much blacker and with a longer tail. Often stands with half-open wings. Seen just as often inland as on the coast.

⟷ 80–100cm

Blackish overall

Long, wide tail

White cheek patch

Short, thick legs

SHAG

Slightly smaller, neater, and snakier than Cormorant, with a rounder head, steeper forehead, and slimmer beak. Strictly a seabird, very rare inland.

⟷ 65–80cm

Greenish black plumage

Wide tail

Short crest

Yellow patch at base of beak

BIRD GALLERY

This colour gallery shows the birds already profiled in the book, grouped by colour. When you see a bird, flick through the colour groupings to find options most like the bird you are watching, then go to their profile page for a closer look. Some birds appear in more than one colour grouping.

Size guide

Birds are grouped in four sizes. Apparent size is more a function of "bulk" than length, so these groups are not precise – but they can help you figure out what you are looking at.

COLOUR GROUP

TINY (House Sparrow)   SMALL (Town Pigeon)

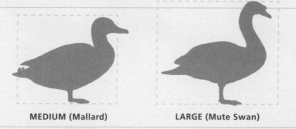

MEDIUM (Mallard)   LARGE (Mute Swan)

Contents

WHITE

Mute Swan
p.77

Whooper Swan
p.77

GREY
For grey-and-white
waders, see pp.120–121

Grey Wagtail
p.89

Wheatear
p.50

Town Pigeon
p.28

Cuckoo
p.41

Hooded Crow
p.47

Mallard ♂
p.62

Gadwall ♂
p.62

Pochard ♂
p.66

Black-headed Gull
p.94

Herring Gull
p.92

Common Gull
p.94

Bewick's Swan
p.77

Little Egret
p.76

White Stork
p.76

Nuthatch
p.39

Woodpigeon
p.28

Stock Dove
p.29

Teal ♂
p.63

Pintail ♂
p.63

Wigeon ♂
p.63

Hen Harrier ♂
p.55

Peregrine
p.55

Grey Heron
p.76

Kittiwake
p.95

Fulmar
p.95

BLACK, WHITE, AND GREY

Goldeneye ♀
p.68

Goosander ♀
p.69

Common Tern
p.98

Arctic Tern
p.98

Sandwich Tern
p.99

Herring Gull
p.92

Yellow-legged Gull
p.93

Lesser Black-backed Gull
p.92

BLACK AND WHITE
For black-and-white waders, see pp.120–121

Coal Tit
p.27

Long-tailed Tit
p.27

House Martin
p.30

Stonechat
p.50

Chaffinch
p.21

Red-breasted Merganser ♂
p.67

Red-breasted Merganser ♀
p.69

Little Tern
p.99

Black-headed Gull
p.94

Mediterranean Gull
p.95

Common Gull
p.94

Kittiwake
p.95

Fulmar
p.95

Pied Flycatcher ♂
p.37

Pied Wagtail
p.89

Grey Wagtail
p.89

Reed Bunting ♂
p.53

Great Spotted Woodpecker
p.38

Jay
p.40

BLACK AND WHITE CONTINUED

Magpie
p.25

Hoopoe
p.40

Great Crested Grebe
p.72

Razorbill
p.101

Puffin
p.100

Oystercatcher
p.81

Lesser Black-backed Gull
p.92

Great Black-backed Gull
p.93

Goosander ♂
p.67

Shoveler ♂
p.62

Shelduck
p.73

Little Egret
p.76

White Stork
p.76

Lapwing
p.78

Black-winged Stilt
p.79

Moorhen
p.73

Guillemot
p.100

Black Guillemot
p.101

Tufted Duck ♂
p.66

Gannet
p.102

Goldeneye ♂
p.66

Eider ♂
p.67

Coot
p.73

Brent Goose
p.75

Canada Goose
p.74

BLACK

Black Redstart
p.19

Swift
p.31

Hooded Crow
p.47

Rook
p.46

Carrion Crow
p.46

Black
Woodpecker
p.38

Shag
p.102

Cormorant
p.102

Tree Pipit
p.48

Rock Pipit
p.48

Pied Wagtail
p.89

Whitethroat
p.51

Pied Flycatcher ♂
p.37

Great Tit
p.26

Blackbird ♂
p.24

Starling
p.24

Jackdaw
p.47

Raven
p.47

Moorhen
p.73

Coot
p.73

WHITE TAIL SIDES

Skylark
p.49

Meadow Pipit
p.48

Grey Wagtail
p.89

Yellow Wagtail
p.89

Mistle Thrush
p.22

Chaffinch
p.21

Linnet
p.53

Reed Bunting ♂
p.53

BROWN: PLAIN
For brown waders,
see pp.120–121

Marsh Tit
p.27

Blackcap
p.34

Pied Flycatcher ♀
p.37

Reed Warbler
p.86

Cetti's Warbler
p.87

Blackbird ♀
p.23

Little Grebe
p.72

Collared Dove
p.29

Dunnock
p.18

Spotted Flycatcher
p.36

House Sparrow
p.18

Rock Pipit
p.48

Skylark
p.49

Crested Lark
p.49

Chaffinch
p.21

Sand Martin
p.31

Swift
p.31

Whitethroat
p.51

Tufted Duck ♀
p.68

Nightingale
p.35

BROWN: STREAKED OR SPOTTED

For brown waders,
see pp.120–121

Wren
p.19

Treecreeper
p.39

Tree Sparrow
p.18

Meadow Pipit
p.48

Tree Pipit
p.48

Woodlark
p.49

Stonechat
p.50

Reed Bunting ♂
p.53

BROWN: STREAKED OR SPOTTED (CONTINUED)

Sedge Warbler
p.87

Grasshopper Warbler
p.86

Reed Bunting ♀
p.88

Yellowhammer
p.52

Song Thrush
p.22

Mallard ♀
p.64

Gadwall ♀
p.64

Shoveler ♀
p.64

Pochard ♀
p.68

Eider ♀
p.69

White-fronted Goose
p.75

Pheasant ♀
p.44

Red-legged Partridge
p.45

Grey Partridge
p.45

Linnet
p.53

Redpoll ♀
p.37

Corn Bunting
p.52

Mistle Thrush
p.22

Redwing
p.23

Fieldfare
p.23

Wigeon ♀
p.65

Teal ♀
p.65

Pintail ♀
p.65

Kestrel
p.54

Sparrowhawk ♀
p.54

Pheasant ♂
p.44

Red Grouse
p.45

Hobby
p.54

Marsh Harrier ♀
p.57

**BROWN:
STREAKED OR
SPOTTED
(CONTINUED)**

Hen Harrier ♀
p.57

Marsh Harrier ♂
p.55

Osprey
p.57

Greylag Goose
p.74

Pink-footed Goose
p.75

Stonechat
p.50

Wheatear
p.50

Whitethroat
p.51

Brambling
p.21

Bullfinch
p.21

Linnet
p.53

Kingfisher
p.88

Waxwing
p.25

Collared Dove
p.29

Buzzard
p.56

Red Kite
p.56

Tawny Owl
p.41

**RED, ORANGE,
PINK,
OR PURPLE**

Robin
p.19

Redstart
p.35

Subalpine Warbler
p.51

Long-tailed Tit
p.27

Chaffinch
p.21

Redpoll ♀
p.36

Crossbill
p.36

Nuthatch
p.39

Turtle Dove
p.29

Jay
p.40

Hoopoe
p.40

GREEN

Goldcrest
p.35

Blue Tit
p.26

Siskin
p.20

Greenfinch
p.20

Yellow Wagtail
p.89

BLUE PATCHES

Blue Tit
p.26

Kingfisher
p.88

RUFOUS ON TAIL/RUMP

Black Redstart
p.19

Redstart
p.35

YELLOW ON WING

Goldfinch
p.20

Siskin
p.20

Great Tit
p.26

Chiffchaff
p.34

Willow Warbler
p.34

Green Woodpecker
p.39

Mallard ♂
p.62

Lapwing
p.78

Swallow
p.30

Great Tit
p.26

Jay
p.40

Nightingale
p.35

Crossbill
p.36

Yellowhammer
p.52

Greenfinch
p.20

Goldcrest
p.35

BROWN WADERS
For other brown birds
see pp.112–117

Snipe
p.80

Golden Plover
p.78

Greenshank
p.81

Redshank
p.81

Curlew
p.82

Little Stint
p.84

Ringed Plover
p.85

Turnstone
p.84

GREY-AND-WHITE WADERS
For other grey birds,
see pp.104–105

Sanderling
p.83

Knot
p.83

BLACK-AND-WHITE WADERS
For other black-and-white birds,
see pp.106–109

Oystercatcher
p.81

Black-winged Stilt
p.79

Green Sandpiper
p.80

Common Sandpiper
p.80

Dunlin
p.83

Black-tailed Godwit
p.82

Bar-tailed Godwit
p.82

Little Ringed Plover
p.85

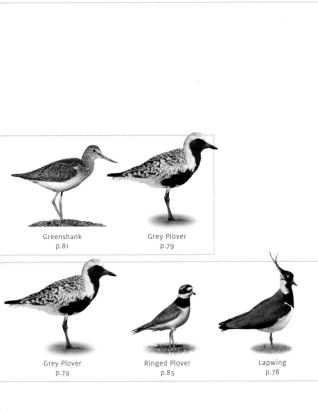

Greenshank
p.81

Grey Plover
p.79

Grey Plover
p.79

Ringed Plover
p.85

Lapwing
p.78

Scientific Names

Every living species has a scientific name of two Latin words. The first word is the genus, shared by closely related species that often look similar. The second is the specific name. Each two-word combination is unique to the individual species.

Common name	Scientific name	Page
Dunnock	*Prunella modularis*	18
House Sparrow	*Passer domesticus*	18
Tree Sparrow	*Passer montanus*	18
Robin	*Erithacus rubecula*	19
Wren	*Troglodytes troglodytes*	19
Black Redstart	*Phoenicurus ochruros*	19
Goldfinch	*Carduelis carduelis*	20
Greenfinch	*Carduelis chloris*	20
Siskin	*Carduelis spinus*	20
Chaffinch	*Fringilla coelebs*	21
Bullfinch	*Pyrrhula pyrrhula*	21
Brambling	*Fringilla montifringilla*	21
Song Thrush	*Turdus philomelos*	22
Mistle Thrush	*Turdus viscivorus*	22
Redwing	*Turdus iliacus*	23
Fieldfare	*Turdus pilaris*	23
Blackbird	*Turdus merula*	23, 24
Starling	*Sturnus vulgaris*	24
Waxwing	*Bombycilla garrulus*	25
Magpie	*Pica pica*	25
Great Tit	*Parus major*	26
Blue Tit	*Cyanistes caeruleus*	26
Coal Tit	*Periparus ater*	27
Long-tailed Tit	*Aegithalos caudatus*	27
Marsh Tit	*Poecile palustris*	27
Town Pigeon	*Columba livia*	28
Woodpigeon	*Columba palumbus*	28
Stock Dove	*Columba oenas*	29
Collared Dove	*Streptopelia decaocto*	29
Turtle Dove	*Streptopelia turtur*	29
Swallow	*Hirundo rustica*	30
House Martin	*Delichon urbicum*	30
Sand Martin	*Riparia riparia*	31
Swift	*Apus apus*	31
Chiffchaff	*Phylloscopus collybita*	34
Willow Warbler	*Phylloscopus trochilus*	34
Blackcap	*Sylvia atricapilla*	34
Nightingale	*Luscinia megarhynchos*	35
Redstart	*Phoenicurus phoenicurus*	35
Goldcrest	*Regulus regulus*	35
Crossbill	*Loxia curvirostra*	36
Redpoll	*Carduelis flammea*	36
Spotted Flycatcher	*Muscicapa striata*	37
Pied Flycatcher	*Ficedula hypoleuca*	37
Black Woodpecker	*Dryocopus martius*	38
Great Spotted Woodpecker	*Dendrocopos major*	38
Green Woodpecker	*Picus viridis*	39

Glossary

Birdwatching has its own jargon. You need to learn very little, and hardly any new words, but a few terms can help you to understand birds better and to describe them with greater precision.

Beak (or bill) Projecting jaws covered with a horny sheath.

Bird of prey A bird that preys on small birds or other animals.

Breeding plumage Plumage in which males display to females in order to mate – often called "summer plumage" but can occur during winter if that is when the birds pair up, as in the case of ducks.

Call (or call note) Short notes used by birds to keep in touch. Louder "flight calls" are helpful in identification, especially of wading birds.

Cap A patch of colour on top of the head.

Covert One of a patch or row of smaller feathers overlying the base of larger wing or tail feathers.

Drake A male duck. ("duck" is then used for the female, but is also used of the whole species in a more general sense.)

Eclipse Dull, female-like plumage of male ducks in summer.

Eye-ring A ring of colour, of either fleshy skin or feathers, around the eye.

Eye-stripe A line of colour through the eye, above the cheeks; a line above the eye is an "eyebrow" or, more correctly, a "superciliary stripe".

Habitat The type of environment a species lives in, providing food, resting sites, and, in summer, nest sites.

Immature A bird that is not yet fully sexually mature.

Juvenile A young bird in its first full covering of feathers.

Migration A regular movement of birds between different geographical areas inhabited at different times of year.

Moult The regular process of shedding and replacing feathers.

Moustache A stripe of colour from the bill, beneath the cheek.

Ornithology The scientific study of birds.

Passage migrant A bird that appears in a certain area only during spring or autumn migration.

Plumage The covering of feathers. Also various overall patterns or colours that identify different ages, sexes, and seasonal changes, such as adult winter or immature female.

Roost To roost (to sleep) or a roost (a place where birds spend the night, or non-feeding periods such as high tide).

Song A particular type of vocal performance that identifies a species, used mostly but not always by males to advertise their presence to others.

Species A "kind" of bird, individuals of which can interbreed and produce fertile, viable young; hybrids between species ("mules") are generally infertile.

Twitching Travelling to try to see a particular bird of a rare species (often a "vagrant", far from its usual range) – not the same as "birdwatching".

Wader A shoreline bird: a plover, sandpiper, or allied species.

Index